Cultural China Series

Lou Qingxi

CHINESE GARDENS

In Search of Landscape Paradise

Translated by Zhang Lei and Yu Hong

CHINA
INTERCONTINENTAL
PRESS

图书在版编目（CIP）数据

中国园林：英文／楼庆西著；张蕾，于红译.—2版.—北京：五洲
传播出版社，2010.1
ISBN 978-7-5085-1663-9

Ⅰ.中... Ⅱ.①楼...②张...③于... Ⅲ.古典园林—简介—中国—
英文 Ⅳ.K928.73
中国版本图书馆CIP数据核字（2009）第180905号

CHINESE GARDENS
In Search of Landscape Paradise

Author: Lou Qingxi
Translator: Zhang Lei and Yu Hong
Polisher: Chen Bingmiao
Executive Editor: Zhang Hong
Art Director: Tian Lin
Production: Primary Colors Design CO.
Publisher: China Intercontinental Press (6 Beixiaomachang, Lianhuachi
    Donglu, Haidian District, Beijing 100038, China)
Tel: 86-10-58891281
Website: www.cicc.org.cn
Printer: C&C Joint Printing Co., (Beijing) Ltd.
Format: 720×965mm 1/16
Edition: Jan. 2010, 2nd edition, 3rd print run
Price: RMB 98.00 (*yuan*)

Contents

Preface

Walking into a Chinese garden, one cannot help but be enchanted by its unique oriental flavor; and walking in an atmosphere of tranquility and peace, one will discover something unlikely to be found in Western architecture—delicate and refined, complex and contained in its quietude. In contrast with natural scenery, the beauty of Chinese gardens lies in their combining culture and art into one. In northern imperial gardens, natural scenes with bridges, creeks and winding paths are interspersed with magnificent palatial architectural groups, fully exemplifying the royal dignity, the most typical of those still existing being the Summer Palace in Beijing. In contrast, private gardens south of the Yangtze River, such as the Lingering Garden, the Humble Administrator's Garden and the Master-of-Nets Garden, play upon their hills, rivers and naturally rich vegetation and achieve a charm not to be found in Northern gardens. These gardens typically belong to government officials, merchants and scholars, serving as part of their private residence, combining living quarters, reception halls and studies with a fascinating array of pavilions, corridors, terrace houses, hills, creeks and vegetation, not large in size but intent on capturing the feeling of natural scenery. The objective of re-creating hills and forests in the city is to show the poetic charm of nature, to draw people away from the maddening crowds, and to seek contentment and peace in nature. These gardens of different nature exemplify a life of stability, contentment and ease, an art of living so to speak. In a sense they reflect the ancient Chinese view of life, of the universe, and the life styles of

Chinese gardens painted by Western painters in early years of the 19Th century

different strata of society and their respective approaches to life, and aesthetic tastes.

In ancient China, from the emperor down to any of the rich, they without exception all took pride in the ownership of a garden in their living space. In the garden one could hold court, entertain guests, hunt, play games, read, play chess, drink tea, chant verses, recite poetry or paint, and over the years a rich garden culture was gradually formed. As more and more scholars and garden owners started participating in the making of gardens, theoretical books on garden building appeared. An outstanding example was the book *Craftsmanship of Gardening* by Ji Cheng (1582–?) in the Ming Dynasty, which discusses the technique of creating a garden as well as garden-related knowledge, experience with garden construction and theories on creating a garden - this book has become a key for people today for an understanding of the Chinese garden concepts. And it is because of the cooperation between scholars and artisans in both theory and technique that the art of the Chinese garden, exemplifying unique Chinese environmental aesthetics, has evolved into a specimen of the classical Chinese culture.

The art of the Chinese garden emphasizes the portrayal of a mood, so that the hills, waters, plants, and buildings as well as their spatial relationship are not just a mere materialistic environment but also evoke a spiritual atmosphere. The builder of the garden, through symbolism and allegories, the search for a poetic mood, the gathering of relics from all over, and the building of temples, streets and even taverns, strives to reach a realm that is natural yet elegant, combining the art of the garden with classical Chinese literature, painting and theatre, where in the true essence of traditional culture lies.

Stone peaks of the Ming Xuan and the half-pavilion built against the wall exhibited i n New York Metropolitan Museum of Art.

The classic Chinese garden, having a long standing artistic and cultural heritage, has also directly influenced the neighboring countries of Korea and Japan. The Japanese garden, having its own unique national traits, has nevertheless continuously absorbed the essence of classic Chinese gardens. On the last day of December 1699, the French court welcomed the coming of the new century with a large Chinese style festival, and a new word "*chinoiserie*" was coined, meaning "of Chinese style". All of a sudden, Chinese ceramics, wallpaper, embroidery, garments, furniture and architecture became all the

The Summer Palace, already listed in World Cultural Heritage, is the largest and best preserved imperial garden in China, and also one of the most well-knowns cenic spots of Beijing.

rage in Europe, as represented by France and England. The art of the Chinese garden spread throughout Europe simultaneously, influencing mostly England and France, but other countries as well, such as Germany, Sweden and Russia, bringing about a transition from geometrical gardens to gardens with natural scenery set-ups.

How did the classic Chinese garden take shape and develop? How many prototypes are there in Chinese gardens, what similarities do they share and how do they differ from each other? What experience has been accumulated through the years of garden building, and what theories have been formed? Let's walk into the Chinese gardens and take a closer look.

Landscape Gardens

The garden should be a perfect blending of nature and construction by man. It should be an imitation of nature, and fully manifest the beauty of nature in limited space; it is also an improvement on nature which should show the painstaking efforts of the garden builder in every corner. The Chinese garden has blended man-made structures like rockery, fish ponds and all manner of pavilions together with flowers, trees, breezes and moonlight of nature, and have combined all these into an artistic entity in which man and nature can co-exist harmoniously.

The presently preserved northern imperial gardens were primarily built in the Ming Dynasty (1368–1644) and the Qing Dynasty (1616–1911), and were places where the feudal royalty could live, enjoy walks in, throw banquets, entertain and hunt. They took up large areas of space and were equipped and decorated very lavishly. The building of these gardens required large amounts of human labor and heavy investments. The gardens of South China are concentrated mostly in cities and towns on the lower reaches of the Yangtze River, which is where scholars loved to gather since ancient times. This is also where writers and calligraphers would live in leisure so they could be close to nature, or where officials and rich merchants would show off their wealth and gamble on horses and dogs. Northern gardens are characterized by grandeur of scope, where as Southern gardens emphasize a more delicate beauty. Famous gardens are scattered all over the Chinese landscape like so many pearls, and give silent testimony to the history and culture of China.

In addition to imperial gardens and private gardens, we can also find open-style scenic areas for the pleasure of the visitor, which possess both the mountains and waters of nature, and cultural spots of interest. These scenic areas are similar in nature to parks, such as the famous five mountain ranges-the Taishan Mountains to the east, The Hengshan Mountains to

The Wu Ling Yuan Scenic Area located in Hunan province of China is a mystic, deep, serene, idyllic world.

the south, the Songshan Mountains on the middle plain area of China, the Huashan Mountains to the west, and the Hengshan Mountains (written differently) to the north. After generations of development and management, these have already become renowned scenic park areas. And the West Lake of Hangzhou is an even more exemplifying model for gardens and parks.

Parks with temples are another lovely form of parks and gardens. The so-called "Temple Parks" refer to parks belonging or attached to Buddhist temples, Taoist temples, altar temples or ancestral halls. The large ones are very much like imperial gardens, whereas the smaller ones resemble more the private gardens. These gardens which are interspersed in natural areas can often be found mixed with parks and gardens of a scenic nature, or are even a part of the scenic parks themselves. Some of the more renowned Temple Parks include Beijing's Tanzhe Temple, Jietai Temple, Taiyuan's Jinci Temple, Suzhou's West Garden, Hangzhou's Lingyin Temple on the West Lake, and Chengde's Waiba (Eight Outer) Temples.

Hunting and Communion with the Spirits

The classic Chinese gardens originate from very ancient times. According to records dating way back to the 21st Century BC, there was already the practice of raising and breeding wild animals for the pleasure of the kings and monarchs' loving of hunting, and these enclosures were known as "You". The kings of the Shang Dynasty (circa.16th–11th Century BC) liked to build high platforms inside the "You" so that they could observe the skies and pay their respects to the gods. These were called Lingtai or spiritual platforms. The platforms were built out of earth, and were of incredibly large size. In "*Xinxu Cishe*" it says-"King Zhou built the deer platform, which took him seven years to complete. It had a length of 3 *li* (note: 1 km=2 *li*) and a height of 1,000 *chi* (note: 1 meter = 3 *chi*), so that he could observe the clouds and rain at his pleasure". This description seems a bit exaggerated, but it is a fact that platforms built in the Shang Dynasty were truly very large and high.

Serving as places for hunting and communion with the spirits were the earliest two functions of the Chinese garden. At the end of the Spring and Autumn Period (722–481 BC), dukes and princes became very numerous, and all the small states began to compete in building palaces, chambers, gardens and platforms. An age of extravagance and hedonism was ushered in, and a change in the nature of the platforms, pavilions and gardens began to take place. Platforms which excluded common people in ancient times did not symbolize the sacred and unattainable anymore. As the form of the state gradually matured, and social activities such as rites, politics and daily life were increasingly clarified, the platforms in gardens did not strive for size and height anymore, but began to form a close structural connection with the surrounding structures. The fog of primitive religion began to slowly disperse, which revealed the innate beauty of the scenery of nature. People began to move away from the blind worship of supernatural powers, and learned to really enjoy and understand the beauty that nature has bestowed us.

The Symbol of a Unified State

In ancient times it was the traditional belief that the powers of the rulers were bestowed on by the gods. Since the power of the emperor came from heaven, the emperor was known as the "Son of Heaven". The Qin Dynasty (221–206 BC) overthrew six smaller states and unified the country, and was later superseded by an even stronger totalitarian Han Dynasty (206 BC– 220 AD). This was the beginning of a consecutive 2,000 years of a unified state with centralized power. The establishment of this form of state government marks a turning point in Chinese history. The influence of this historic period on the art of gardening was also deep

Potrait of Qinshihuang, the first emperor in China's history

and profound.

From historic annals dating from the Qin and Han periods, we can see many records of large-scale architectural building and construction of gardens during this period which roughly covered 400 years. In the year 221 BC, the Emperor Qinshihuang unified the country and set up a vast feudal empire. He ordered 200 thousand rich families to move to Xianyang in Shaanxi Province, in order to centralize manpower and resources so he could implement his ambitious construction plan. The Qin Dynasty palace is of astoundingly large proportions. The most famous Qin Dynasty palace is the E-fang Palace which was built south of the capital of that time, Xianyang. In the "Annals of History-Section on Emperor Qinshihuang", is written the following passage..."the front palace of E-fang is 500 paces from east to west, and 50 *zhang* (note: one *zhang* equals 10 Chinese feet) from south to north. It is large enough to hold 10 thousand people, and tall enough to erect a 5-*zhang* banner". Emperor Qinshihuang used the Xianyang Palace as the center, and around in a radius extending for scores of miles planned to build over 200 palaces and chambers, which were all to be mutually connected by passageways above the ground. This made this whole region both his palace area and his garden area. This extravagant construction plan was never completed. The Qin Dynasty only lasted 13 years, and the dream of Emperor Qinshihuang of building an empire that would last down the ages went up in flames together with the fire that razed E-fang Palace. It is said that the fire raged for 3 months before E-fang Palace was finally burnt down to the ground.

After the fall of the Qin Empire, the former capital of Xianyang fell into ruins. The Western Han Dynasty (206 BC–25 AD) set up its capital in the City of Chang'an, which lies to the southeast of Xianyang. The palaces of Western Han were also very large in scope. Of palaces in Chang'an city, the Changle Palace and

Quiet and simple rural scenery portrayed in the famous East Jin painting *The Ode of Luo Deity*.

Weiyang Palace alone took up one third of the whole area of the city. If you add some of the smaller palaces such as Gui Palace, Bei (North) Palace and Mingguang Palace, the palace area took up over one half of the whole city, whose area proper was 36 square kilometers. This is over 20 times the space occupied by the Forbidden City of the Ming and Qing Dynasties, which took up approximately 0.72 square kilometer.

The power of the Han Dynasty and its garden construction both reached their peak during the reign of the Emperor Han Wu (140–87 BC). In order to show the absolute authority of the emperor, Emperor Han Wu personally oversaw the construction of gardens. The Shanglin Yuan (Upper Woods Garden) is situated south of Chang'an, starting north from the southern banks of the Wei River and terminating at the foot of the Zhongnan Mountains. It is surrounded by a wall of approximately 130-

160 kilometers, which includes the northern slopes of Zhongnan Mountains and the southern slopes of Jiujun Mountains. The eight largest rivers of central Shaanxi all run from north to south through the garden. Just the Kunming Pond alone, which was dug with manual labor, has an area of 150 hectares, which is quite sufficient for navy training activities. Inside the garden are 12 clusters of buildings, and the garden is also complete with paths, covered corridors, bridges and pavilions, which completed the sense of changes in space. There were separate palaces and gardens for the cultivation of flowers and plants, enjoyment of music, dog racing and the planting of weeping willows, all for

The Goose Playing Pond in the Orchid Pavilion in Shaoxing, an ancient garden where East Jin calligrapher Wang Xizhi watched geese and created calligraphic work.

the pleasure of the emperor. Outside of the palace, you could also find 36 smaller "gardens within gardens". In the Shanglinyuan (Upper Woods Garden) were cultivated all manner of fruit trees and trees for their beauty, to say nothing of the multitudes of rare fowls and animals. It is no exaggeration to say that this was at the same time a large botanical garden, zoo, and plantation. The Western Han historian Sima Xiangru when describing the Shanglinyuan Garden wrote with exaggeration: the most southern stretches of the garden still flourish with vegetation in the winter, whereas the most northern stretches of the garden are frozen over with ice and snow in the summer. The Shanglinyuan Garden is the largest scale garden to be found throughout Chinese history, and gardens of this size were rarely found in later times.

The Shanglinyuan Gardens, like the E-fang Palace, was also destroyed by the ravage of war. But it had a tremendous lasting influence on the art of garden construction in later times. To symbolize a large and unified country, the palaces and parks of both the Qin and Han Dynasties all strived to manifest the heavens, the earth and the universe in their design. The tremendous amount of land area and space they occupied and the great diversity of the buildings and landscapes were the basic prerequisite behind the thoughts guiding their design, and fully manifested the political views and interpretation of the universe at that time. And in the Taiye Pond in the Shanglin yuan Garden were built three islands, which signify the three sacred mountains of Yingzhou of the Eastern Seas, Penglai and Fangzhang which can be found in folk tales. This practice of building 3 sacred mountains in a body of water was passed down as a classic tradition to builders of gardens of later times, and we can find this theme of "three mountains in a pond" repeatedly.

Fully Enjoying the Beauty of Nature

Beginning from the fall of the Eastern Han Dynasty (26–220 AD), China entered a period of divided rule and constant fighting among smaller states, which lasted around 300 years. This was a time of great social upheaval. The rise and fall of different states and the succession of dynasties was like a constantly shifting lantern show before the eyes. Normal production was disturbed, the economy came to a standstill, and the population decreased sharply. On the other hand, in the area of ideology, the tradition of Confucianism as the only ruling thought was challenged. Confucianism, Taoism and Buddhism contended for the upper hand on the ideological scene which became much livelier. The unique "Wei and Jin Style" which we can find in the history of China's culture pertains to the cultural and spiritual characteristics of this period.

During the Wei-Jin and South-North Dynasties (220–586 AD), sociopolitical contradictions were very sharp. The social strata of the officials became very disillusioned with their future as officials and with life in general. This gave rise to a philosophy of seeking peace and quiet and doing nothing that goes against nature. It became fashionable to talk idly of metaphysics and other mysterious matters. What is more, in 67 AD Buddhism was introduced into China and this exerted a profound influence on the thought of that time. The officials of the time combined the Buddhist and the Taoist escapist attitude, and chose a lifestyle of distancing themselves from the centers of political power, losing themselves in the beauty of nature, and giving no regard to their personal appearance, so that they could both keep out of political trouble and pride themselves in the cultivation of personality. At the same time, a new form of production organization began to develop rapidly from out of the traditional Chinese feudal economic structures-the plantation. This type

The ancient painting named *Guo Country Ladies' Field Trip in Spring* recreates the happy life when Tang Dynasty's noble ladies played and enjoyed themselves freely in outskirts of the city.

of self-sufficient economic structure ensured the independence and creativity of the official strata in the realm of ideology and culture. In addition to fully enjoying walking among natural scenic spots, they also tried to emulate this scenery of forests and hills on the grounds of their own residences to create an idyllic and pastoral atmosphere of nature in the wild that they could enjoy at will. Thus the early stage of the private garden appeared on the scene. The distinguishing feature of this type of garden was that natural things like hills, bodies of water such as ponds and streams, and vegetation made up the main structure of this garden landscaping system. Due to the limitations of geographic, climatic and economic conditions, the practice of using man-made rocks made from materials obtained nearby took place of the practice of building gardens next to large mountains of the

Qin and Han dynasties. The plants most commonly used were pine, fir and bamboo. These were selected because they are green all year round, and are also tall and straight, which was used to symbolize the upright character of the owner. In the private gardens of that time, the spatial relationship of objects and plants became even more intricate and exquisite.

Using Luoyang, the capital of Northern Wei (386–584 AD) as an example, there were 220 small residential districts and large numbers of private gardens were built within these districts. According to records of the "Luoyang Jialan Records", at that time Luoyang was rich in hydraulic resources. To take the gardens of the high-ranking official Zhang Lun as example, in his garden you could find lawns and trees and he tried to emulate nature in the wild. There was an imitation of the famous Jing Yang Mountain, the trees were tall enough to block out the heat of the sun, and vines swayed gently with the breezes. We can see

The famous Tang Dynasty garden recreated by the Qing Dynasty painters-*Luchai*, Wang Wei's villa in Wangchuan.

that people of that time already knew how to duplicate natural scenery in their own homes. In these gardens not only were there magnificent buildings, but these were ingeniously combined with natural hills and waters to form complete landscapes. This method of utilizing hills and waters in garden construction, and emphasizing the elegance and details of the structure of the buildings, painstakingly selecting trees and plants, and cutting out winding paths leading to beautiful shaded places were exemplary models that garden builders of later times all liked to imitate.

The imperial gardens of this time were primarily built inside the palace grounds of each state. To take the Three Kingdom Period (220–280 AD) as an example, in the capital of the Wei Kingdom Ye Cheng City (the northern part of Anyang, Henan Province today) was built the Bronze Peacock Garden. In Luoyang of Northern Wei was built the Hualin Gardens and the Xiyou Gardens, and in the capital of the Southern Dynasty Jiankang (today Nanjing of Jiangsu Province) was built the Hualin Gardens and the Leyou Gardens. These imperial gardens were comprised mainly of hills, ponds and streams, all kinds of vegetation, and different types of pavilions. They no longer possessed the functions of hunting and merrymaking as imperial gardens of earlier periods did. In the gardens were built small-scale hills symbolic of the five greater mountains, as well as lakes and islets. The buildings and structures were adorned with carved or painted rafters, and had protruding eaves or roof corners that were tilted upwards. Some were built directly on the water, and some were connected by long corridors or bridges. All of this served to enhance the majestic and extravagant style of the imperial gardens built in the midst of natural surroundings.

Simultaneous with the development of the art of garden building during this period was the flourishing of the culture of the literati (intelligentsia and ranked officials) including

Nine Dragon Pond in Lintong, Shaanxi province - scenic garden built on the original site of Tang Dynasty temporary palace.

poetry and literature, calligraphy, painting, music, culinary arts and clothing and jewelry. All of the above was developed to an unprecedented level. People of later times spoke highly of Chinese classic gardens as blending natural scenery together with poetry, calligraphy and painting, and this style of garden construction actually began from this period.

Together with the building of Buddhist and Taoist temples all over China was the emergence of many temple gardens, which gradually merged together with imperial gardens and privately-owned gardens. The imperial gardens of this period no longer possessed the splendor of gardens of the Qin and Han period. Chinese gardens beginning from this period discarded the grandiose and large-scale style of earlier periods, and began to develop the small and exquisite style of later times.

Gardens of Pleasure in Prosperous Times

In the Year 581, the establishment of the Sui Dynasty (581–618 AD) put an end to the long period of divided rule in China. 37 years later, the Tang Dynasty (618–907 AD) overthrew the Sui Dynasty, and set up a great unified feudal empire. Because the Tang rulers adopted a policy of developing production and stabilizing society as a whole, agriculture developed, the economy flourished and the whole political situation was stabilized. China became prosperous as never before.

If the love of natural surroundings of the Wei and Jin period reflected the disillusionment with politics and the need to escape from reality, then, on the contrary, the same love of natural-style gardens of the Tang Dynasty was based on the need for recreation and pleasure of the flourishing rule at that time. The imperial gardens of the Tang Dynasty were mainly concentrated in the city proper and suburban areas of the capital Chang'an and the eastern capital Luoyang. The largest of these gardens was Jin Yuan (the Forbidden Garden) situated on the north side of Chang'an. In the Annals of Chinese History, it is recorded that it was 27 *li* (13.5 km) in width from east to west, and 23 *li* (11.5 km) in length from north to south, and covered a very large area. Inside the garden could be found 24 smaller gardens and clusters of structures, such as the Wangchun (Looking to Spring) Palace, Yuzao (Fish and Weed) Palace, Jiuqu (Nine Turns) Pond, and Fangya (Letting out the Duck) Pavilion. Jin Yuan was the main place where royalty would come to enjoy the scenery and for hunting. Every year, the emperor would come with the empress, his concubines and his subjects for hunting, feasting, singing and dancing, games, soccer, cock-fights, and rope-pulling contests. These are just some examples of the various games and entertainment in the gardens. Polo was especially popular among the Tang Dynasty emperors, at which they became very adept. During the mid-Tang period, a Royal Art Institute was set up in the Liyuan (Pear) Garden at the southern tip of the Jinyuan Gardens. The emperor of that time, Li Longji (date of rule 712– 755 AD), personally taught music at the Institute.

The palace gardens of the Tang Dynasty had "three inners"(the Daming Palace, the Taiji Palace and the Xingqing Palace), and "three gardens" (the Dongnei Garden, the Xinei Garden and the Jinyuan Garden). The so-called "three inners" were primarily a combination of palaces and gardens. The frontal part of the

Royalgardens in Bianjing portrayed in the Song Dynasty painting *Jinming Pond Contest*

Daming Palace was the palace area and the north of this area was the garden area. In the center of the Daming Palace area was the Taiyechi, a pond of vast dimensions, which was situated on the same central axis as the Xuande (Advocate Virtue) Palace and the Zichen (Royal Purple) Palace. This way of situating the palace area in the front and the garden area in the rear became the basic layout of royal palace of future times.

The Quyang Pond at the south-east corner of Chang'an was also known as the Furong or Hibiscus Garden. This garden was originally reserved for the pleasure of the royalty, and not until later was it opened to the public. The banks of the pond are full of curves and inlets, with different styles of pavilions built on the edges of the bank, and trees and flowers of all sorts planted there to please the eye, making it one of the most beautiful scenic garden spots in Chang'an. Every year on the third day of the third month and the ninth day of the ninth month of the lunar calendar, the garden is decorated with festive lanterns and colored streamers, music is played throughout the garden, and merchants and vendors selling all manner of goods set up stalls along the banks. The emperor comes with the emperess and his concubines to enjoy themselves in the garden, and he lays out feasts for all the officials. On these days, ordinary folk are also admitted to the garden, which makes it a medley of crowds, color and joy. This practice of making the imperial gardens into places where common people can also enjoy themselves together with the royalty and aristocrats is very rarely found throughout the whole history of Chinese feudal society.

It is noteworthy that the flourishing of culture and art during the Tang Dynasty created a very favorable cultural background for the development of private gardens. The depictions of natural scenery in Tang period poetry became not only more numerous, but also increasingly mature. The traditional Chinese scenic paintings also not only gradually matured but became an independent school of painting in itself, and many renowned scenic painters of that period became famous in later times. The flourishing of poetry and painting depicting scenery, together with its creative methods, exerted an important influence on the designing and building of gardens of that period. To take the Wangchuan Garden Residence built near Chang'an by the famous poet and painter Wang Wei as an example-he built this garden in a natural valley endowed with hills, forests and lakes. This garden has 20 scenic spots. The scenery is extremely picturesque, and inspired a good number of his better-known poems. Although this garden is no longer in existence, people of later times still continue to sing its praises. Emperor Qianlong of the Qing Dynasty (reign from 1736 to 1795) even built a "Beiyuan Mountain Village" scenic spot in the Yuanmingyuan Garden in imitation of Wang Wei's Wangchuan Garden Residence.

The literati of prosperous times seemed to possess especially high spirits. The famous poet Bai Juyi personally designed and constructed a garden residence in Luoyang City, and would frequently invite his friends in the literary circle to come there for drinking, singing, conversing on literature and poetry and enjoying themselves in general. Every autumn when the weather became cool and pleasant, he would come to the garden to drink and play musical instruments. After he got drunk, he would have young boys construe to play music for him in the pavilions on the pond, and the sound of the music would mingle with the mist of the lake. The poet also built a so-called "Lushan Mountain Grass House" on the north of the Xianglu (Incent Burner) Peak of Lushan Mountian in Jiangxi Province. The walls were made of mud, and the window frames of wood, with paper for window panes, and hanging bamboo shades and curtains. No paint at all was used, giving it a natural and simple style. Inside the garden could be found tall ancient pines and cool bamboo forests. The mountain rocks were ingeniously arranged, and the pleasant sound of the waterfall could be heard at all times.

Gardens built by men of letters reflected their general philosophy of life. Their style was mainly clear, fresh, simple and elegant, as compared with the extravagance and luxury of the imperial gardens and the splendor and ornate style of the privately owned gardens of the officials. The development of the gardens of the intelligentsia during the Tang period laid a solid foundation for the rules by which such gardens were built in later times.

A World in a Wine Pot

Garden building developed to even further heights during the Song Dynasty (960–1279). In addition to imperial gardens, private gardens and temple gardens, even teahouses and pubs in cites would embellish their surroundings with gardens with ponds and rockery in order to attract customers.

The Genyue Garden was built in Bianliang (today's Kaifeng of Henan Province), the east capital of the Song Dynasty. It is the most well-known, as well as the most representative of all the imperial gardens of the Song Dynasty. In comparison with the vast expanses of land (up to several hundred li) that the gardens of the Han and Tang periods occupied, the actual area of the Genyue Garden was only about a dozen li, and the highest hill took less than a hundred steps to climb. However, Genyue Garden occupies an important place in the history of classic Chinese gardens. It is reputed to be "the most beautiful under the heavens, and the most excellent of all times". How was it possible to create a garden of such exquisite beauty on such a relatively small piece of land? Putting it into a few words, the secret lay in "concentration of scenery", in other words, trying to combine hills, ponds and streams, palaces and temples, rural cottages, and flowers and trees into one in a limited space, to achieve a multilayered and three dimensional effect. It encompasses the scenery of Jianhu Lake of Shaoxing City, the Feilai Peak of Hangzhou, the Tao Xi (Peach Creek) written of by writer Tao Yuanming (365–427) and the Meichi (Plum) Pond written of by Lin Bu (967–1028), renowned for his paintings of plum blossoms. There is also the legendary "Baxian Guan (Hall of Eight Immortals)" and the rural houses and beautiful village scenery. All of the parts making up the garden blend into each other naturally, and possess an artistic style which is natural, simple, peaceful and introspective. Walking through the garden, you see a different scene with each step you go into the garden the more of its beauty becomes apparent. From small scenes you can envision larger scenes. This is a man-made natural scenic garden that concentrates hills, ponds, streams and the most lush and gorgeous vegetation into one. This 'in the pond' model, which began to appear in the mid to late Tang Dynasty, was carried on and further developed during the Song Period, reaching new pinnacles of maturity and artistic perfection. The gardens of the intelligentsia of this time occupied much less space than those of previous times, but in the relatively small courtyards could be found brooks, hills, springs, ponds, islets, trees, flowers, rocks, pavilions and halls-in short, just about anything you could think of for a garden. Inside the small space of the "wine pot", you could find artificial hills, ponds and streams, rocks and cultivated flowers and vegetation which were not only ingeniously combined but also ever-changing in their artistic effect, as well as structures exquisite and delicate in design. You can well imagine what difficulties this re-creation of the ever-changing scenes found in nature presented to the designers of these gardens. But people of the Song Dynasty took the art of garden design to new heights of perfection with their unprecedented creativity and artistic talent. This was also the period when China's traditional aesthetic spirit developed to its highest achievement.

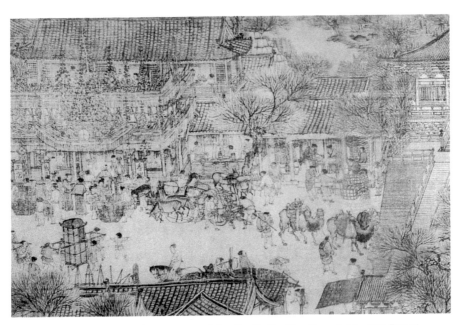

Tavern gardens portrayed in the Song Dynasty painting *The Bustling River Scene in Qingming Festival*

The privately owned gardens of the Song Period, including large numbers of those belonging to officials, eunuchs and men of letters, were largely concentrated in Kaifeng, Luoyang, Suzhou and Hangzhou. These gardens were also the most representative of this period. The small garden art pieces of this time, such as scrolls with couplets, horizontally inscribed plaques, stone foundations with inlaid patterns, column bases, indoor and outdoor potted landscapes, goldfish tanks and paving, which were both decorative and complimentary to the whole garden, not only surpassed previous periods in their richness and diversity, but also included many pieces of exceeding beauty which was not to be paralleled in later times.

This period which lasted over three hundred years was the period of maturing in the development of China's classical garden. During this period, the government-compiled book

Ying Fa Zao Shi described in detail the architectural concept "cai fen zhi", from which we get to learn the basic laws governing ancient architectural design. It is a highly perfected modulus system, which shows that China's wood structure architecture had already developed to a mature stage. From the paintings of the Song Period we can also see the great diversity of types and forms of architectural structures of this period. Their exquisite beauty and delicate style are entirely different from the grand and sweeping style of the structures of the Tang Period.

A Vision to Move the Heaven and Condense the Earth

China's feudal society entered the Ming(1368–1644) and Qing Dynasties (1644–1911) from the Yuan Dynasty. Freehand style of Chinese landscape painting reached its maturity in the Yuan Dynasty, accelerating the development and perfection of the art of garden building. And the all-round development of imperial gardens, private gardens, temple gardens and natural scenery gardens led to the building of Yuanmingyuan (Garden of Perfect Splendor), a representative work of the later years of ancient China's gardens, when the art of garden building further developed into a unique garden design theory.

Imperial gardens of the Ming Dynasty surround the Wansui Mountain and the Taiye Pond, as represented by the West Garden inside the Royal City Proper, and the Yuhuayuan (Royal Garden) within the Forbidden City. Both imperial gardens and privately-owned gardens of the Qing Dynasty had their unique contributions, and they form the main body of the classical Chinese gardens we see today. We can take as an example the Bishu Shanzhuang (Mountain Estate for Escaping the Heat) built in Chengde north of the Great Wall. It is a combination of architectural styles of the Han, the Mongolian and the Tibetan

The serene North Sea Park in Beijing (shot in the early years of the 20ᵗʰ century)

people, with a combination of various religious architecture rarely seen either inside or outside of China. In addition, the scenery varies by region, with the lake areas portraying the exquisite charm of the river villages of south China, the hills areas showing the unconstrained and rugged beauty of mountainous west China, and the flatland area showing a unique lush style north of the Great Wall. It is a "museum of garden art" indeed. Westerners who have had a comprehensive view of the Garden of Perfect Splendor call it the "garden of ten thousand gardens", as it not only absorbed the essence of the art of gardening throughout all the dynasties, but also drew on the architectural styles of the West, perfect examples of which are the Baroque style water fountain and Western-style mansion at the north of

Changchun Yuan Garden. The art of Chinese gardens, over a long period of development and perfection, has now encompassed the contemporary spirit of east-west exchange.

Private gardens of the Qing Dynasty are mainly concentrated in the area of Nanjing, Suzhou and Yangzhou, with the Yangzhou gardens being the most representative. The Geyuan Garden of Yangzhou has hills in the garden and pavilions on the hills, and from the pavilion you can see the entire city proper covered in green, the magnificent scenery of the Slender West Lake and Pingshantang Hall, showing a highly developed art of garden construction.

Private Gardens of Ming and Qing Dynasties

Private gardens of the Ming and Qing Dynasties are mainly situated south of the Yangtze River (traditionally referring to the plain at the lower reaches of the Yangtze River), a rich and populous region with a long cultural heritage, and in Beijing, the political center of that time. In the ancient southern city of Suzhou alone there were already over 170 gardens by the beginning of the 20th century, 60 of which remain fully preserved today. Each garden is an all-encompassing piece of artwork made up of architecture, hills and streams, as well as lush vegetation and flowers, combining the beauty of natural scenery, of architectural forms, and of landscape paintings. They are not only specimens of gardens all over China, but also the world's precious cultural heritage. Take a casual stroll in Suzhou—the "city of gardens", and from the bridges, creeks and ancient gardens you can catch a glimpse of the face of history.

Private Gardens of the South

Private gardens south of the Yangtze River are represented by those of Suzhou, Yangzhou, Wuxi, Zhenjiang and Hangzhou.

The picture shows the Slender West Lake in Yangzhou.

(left) The delicate view-finding gate in South China scholar's garden
(top) Water pavilion in the garden
(bottom)The View-watching pavilion connecting the outer corridor

During the Ming and Qing periods, the feudal culture reached its peak in Suzhou, and the art of garden construction reached maturity. A large number of garden artists appeared, and the practice of garden construction flourished. Gardens in Suzhou, with their intricacy and precision of design, reflect a mood created from nature but surpassing nature, a mood unique to Chinese culture. Out of these gardens, the Lion Forests, the Humble Administrator's Garden, the Lingering Garden, the Master-of-Nets Garden and the Canglang Pavilion have been listed as the World Cultural Heritage by UNESCO. Gardens in

Yangzhou were mostly residential gardens, scattered all along streets and alleys in their prime times, and are easily found along suburban river banks. By the Qianlong Period of the Qing Dynasty, the famous "Slender West Lake" garden area was already formed, with its famous 24 scenes. Yangzhou was the proud owner of more gardens than Suzhou, and was renowned for "having the best of gardens under heaven." Unfortunately, most gardens were destroyed in the turmoil of war times. Hangzhou owns the famous West Lake garden area, where gardens are centered around the West Lake. Each garden has a different theme, and the one most representative of the beauty of Chinese gardens is the Guozhuang Garden built in 1907, which was called the "number one garden of the West Lake." People of that time enjoyed constructing gardens, and liked to link gardens with one's personal character: it was said that when making gardens the ideal is to be winding, but when making friends, one should be straight.

Conditions under which Southern Private Gardens were Built

It is not a coincidence that private gardens since the Ming and Qing Dynasties are mainly concentrated south of the Yangtze River. It is here where all prerequisites for garden construction are met, be it natural settings, economic conditions or development in the humanities.

The flourishing of private gardens in the south would not be possible without its advantageous natural conditions. First of all, the south is rich in rivers and lakes, and the hydraulic network and abundant water supply make it easy to bring water into the garden. Situated in the temperate zone, there is no severe cold weather in winter, and the high humidity is ideal for evergreen vegetation and a large variety of plants and flowers. Therefore gardens in the south commonly have lush vegetation of great

The natural scenery in the East Lake Scenic garden in Shaoxing variety. This area is also home to rocks and stones ideal for garden construction. In this manner, all resources used for water works, hills, construction and vegetation are realized locally.

The south is more populous in both rural and urban areas in comparison with the north. Due to the advantages in climate, soil, produce and natural resources as well as the unique geographical location, the south has enjoyed the reputation of being the "land of abundant fish and rice" since ancient times, and holds a pivotal position in China's economic structure. By the Ming and Qing Dynasties, southern China was undisputedly the most prosperous area in the nation with highly developed agriculture, handicrafts and commerce.

The economic prosperity of urban and rural areas in southern China gave an impetus to the sustained development of architecture, and promoted progress in architectural material and technology. A long period in architectural practice created a large number of craftsmen, who had long been famous for their outstanding skills in carpentry, bricklaying and plastering, and these men were often sent for construction work at the Royal Palace. In the Ming and Qing Dynasties, many outstanding craftsmen in northern China came from the south, although the architectural techniques and styles of the north and the south are distinctly different.

Garden construction is a form of cultural construction, which requires not only material availability but also needs to be deeply rooted in a rich soil of humanities. Southern China has a long and profound Han cultural heritage, which historically produced countless outstanding figures. Meanwhile the highly developed economy and culture as well as the prosperous urban lifestyle all attracted literati from other regions. Famous poets such as Bai Juyi and Su Shi had both served as local administrator of Hangzhou, undertaking the renovation of the West Lake, clearing the sludge, constructing the long embankment, planting in the lake area and building scenic spots to make the West Lake a scenic garden area. Meanwhile they both wrote a large number of beautiful poems in praise of the West Lake, thus adding to the cultural heritage of the area.When the Southern Song Dynasty (1127–1279) had its capital moved to Lin'an (now Hangzhou, Zhejiang), many government officials and scholars followed. They chanted poems and painted, giving rise to a trend of artistic creation in the south, and the most popular were landscape poetry and paintings, both of which had a direct impact on the art of garden construction.

Natural, economic and artistic advantages paved the way for the development of the art of the garden. Since the Southern Song Dynasty, large numbers of government officials, rich merchants and scholars gathered in the Suzhou and Hangzhou area, bringing about the trend of garden construction. In the Ming and Qing Dynasties, government officials were selected through the imperial examination system, and many were selected from the south and sent to Be.ing. Upon retirement these scholars and officials would return to their hometown, purchasing land and building gardens. For these reasons, southern private gardens in the Ming and Qing Dynasties reached their peak in terms of both quantity and quality.

Famous Gardens of the South

Jichang Garden of Wuxi

The Jichang Garden of Wuxi is a famous hillside residence garden in the south, well known for its meticulous work in construction and unique artistic style. The Jichang Garden has a history of over 400 years, initially serving as the residence of Qin Yao, Minister of the Board of War of the Xuande Period (1506–1521), Ming Dynasty. By the 19th Year of the Wanli Period (1591), descendants of Qin Jin remodeled the residence into

Jichang Garden, and the garden has been remodeled several times over since. The garden not only has the southern garden's typical charm and grace of re-created nature, but also stands out with unique appeal by cleverly blending the garden into nature and building it against the hills.

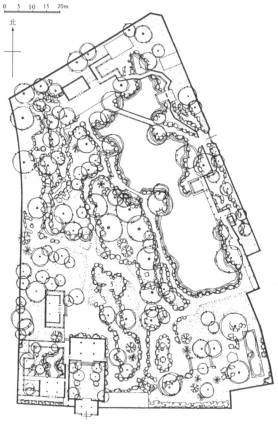

Walking into the west side of Jichang Garden, ancient trees, secluded valleys and the sound of the springs gives you the illusion of the nature in wild, and you see artificial hills everywhere, taking up as much as two thirds of the entire area. Planted on the hills are trees and bushes, and valleys and gullies run along the shape of the hills. Springs led in from Huishan Mountain drop from all levels of the slopes, singing and tinkling to form the scene of the "music box gully".

The ichnography of the Jichang Garden in Wuxi

At the east of the garden lies a pond, narrow shaped with the long sides on the north and south and the narrow sides on the east and west. The pond takes up as much as 17% of the total garden area, and is called "Jin Hui Yi (Ripple of the Pooled Brocade)". The water is divided into two areas of north and south, breaking up the monotony by a long stretch of water. At the north of the pond there are flat bridges and covered bridges across the water, adding visual interest to a not-so-big water area.

Canglang Ting
Located at Canglang Ting Street on southern part of Suzhou city and covered an area of 1.1 hectare, Canglang Pavilion was one of big-scale gardens in Suzhou city and also the garden with longest history in Suzhou. The garden featured a style of garden making popular in the Song dynasty, also a sample of gardens imitating art of freehand landscape painting. It first belonged to jiedushi (a high-ranking military title) Sun Chengyou, a close relative to the king of Wuyue nation in the Wudai dynasty. In 1045 (Northern Song dynasty), a wandering poet named Su Sunqin bought the garden with 40 thousand qian and built a pavilion upon the waterside and named it Canglang Pavilion. The garden passed through a number of owners, was remodeled and enlarged for several times. The existing Canglang Pavilion was a historic site reconstructed in 1873 of the Qing dynasty.

Finally, a "water tail" is built at the very northern end, and camouflaged by a covered bridge, the water giving the illusion of having a source without an end. Although limited in size, the Jin Hui Yi is nevertheless full of visual interests and does not seem at all cramped with its winding riverbanks and multiple levels of water partition.

In comparison with the hills and water, the architecture does not seem to be much. Except for a few temples, ancestral halls and chambers near the entrance, the other few pavilions, platforms, towers and bridges are all scattered around the pond. The Fish Watching Fence at the mid section on the eastern bank of the pond protrudes into the water and becomes the visual center of the entire pond, from where a full view of the hills on the western bank can be Private Gardens of Ming and Qing Dynasties obtained. The Jiashu Hall at the north of the garden is built on a high and open space, serving as the main

Knowing Fish House is the center of the water scene design of the Jichang Garden.

view of the entire garden-looking up from there the Huishan Mountain can be seen standing on the opposite side, and looking back there is the Xishan Mountain and the shadow of its pagodas. Watching the spring ripples before the eyes, it seems virtually like a walk in a painting. Although the Xishan and Huishan Mountains are not in the gardens, the view far exceed if they were in the garden. The mere two and half mu of the narrow land is a feast for the eye with layer after layer of scenery without end.

The Jichang Garden in Wuxi - the greenness coming into your eyes through the door opening

Because of its clearly defined plans, with meticulous attention paid to the styles of hills, rocks and ponds, as well as treatment of architectural details, scenes of unique beauty have been created within limited sphere. What is especially noteworthy is that the garden's mountain and woods environment, with heavy and dense hills and water highlighted with scattered buildings, have fully inherited the intellectual garden style since the Tang and Song Dynasties and thus deserves to be rated as top-grade garden of the Ming and Qing Dynasties.

The Humble Administrator's Garden

The Humble Administrator's Garden is another outstanding private garden of southern China. The garden is situated at the north-eastern part of the city of Suzhou, and was first built in the Zhengde Period (1506–1521) of the Ming Dynasty. The garden is divided into eastern, central and western parts, which altogether add up to 4.1 hectares in area, which is quite large for private

Ting

The hall in a garden is a structure catering to the need of entertaining visitors, dining, appreciating plants or small performances, functioning as a public facility in ancient gardens. It has some specific requirements. It should be large enough to include a great number of visitors. The overall modeling of the structure should be elegant and dignified, emphasizing exquisite ornaments for doors and windows. Plenty of flowers and trees should be erected before the hall as well as rockeries. Normally windows and doors are only put up in the front and back of the hall, but in some cases they are erected in each side of the hall.

gardens. Up to now the central and western sections have retained their original appearance, whereas the eastern part has been remodeled into a new garden. Although the current the Humble Administrator's Garden is not quite the same as the one in the Zhengde Period of the Ming Dynasty, it still serves as a good example of ancient Chinese private gardens.

The central part of the Humble Administrator's Garden is the main part of the garden, and in terms of overall planning, this part can be divided into the northern water area and the southern land area, each of which takes up half of the total space. The southern area is where the majority of the architecture and where the major halls, principal rooms, towers and houses are located. In terms of scenery area arrangements, this part can be divided into three areas from east to west, with the central part being the most important. The Yuanxiang (Distant Fragrance) Hall at center of the garden is the largest hall type architecture of the entire garden. Built facing the water, the hall has a wide and open terrace at the north, from where the

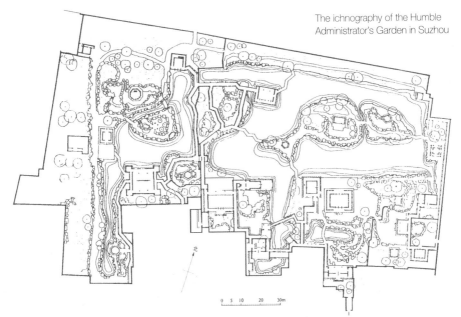

The ichnography of the Humble Administrator's Garden in Suzhou

北

0 5 10   20   30m

best view of the lotus feasts the eyes. The Distant Fragrance Hall is decorated with French doors, and through the windows the hills and waters all can be seen like a scroll of scenic paintings. The eastern area is made up of a group of architecture including Haitang Chun Wu (Spring Crabapple Flower Dock), the Linglong House (Exquisite Garden), etc. It is an area enclosed within walls and artificial hills, with loquat trees planted within, and the area is therefore called "Loquat Garden". The western area holds the Yulan Tang (Magnolia Hall), Dezhen (Attainment of Truth) Pavilion and Xiangzhou (Fragrant Islet) Stone Bridge inside an open courtyard space formed with corridors and artificial hills.

The central part of the Humble Administrator's Garden is mainly a scenic area of open waters, with complimentary architectural scenes. The water and the architecture together form a garden area of infinite beauty. The northern area of the central part of the garden is the water scene area, and built within the water are two islets on which hills are built with earth and stone. On the western islet at the top of the hill is built a Fragrant Snow and Clouds Pavilion. On the western end of the islet there is a pavilion named "Lotus Breeze from all Sides", named for the lotuses around it. Viewed from above, the Pavilion of "Lotus Breeze from all Sides", rises out of the water with upturned eaves, like a pearl surrounded with a pond full of lotuses. On the eastern islet there is the Pavilion of the Northern Hills. Flat bridges are built between the two islets and between each islet and the water bank, and the bridges serve both for the convenience of the tourists and to add to the variety and coherence of the water scenes. Northwest central part, although an area concentrated with architecture, has a variety of architectural forms of halls, mansions, pavilions and stone bridges interspersed with corridors, bridges and artificial hills, and decorated with crabapple flower trees and loquat trees. The garden scenes therefore give no sense of monotony, but rather a

Interior scene of the Liuting Storied Pavilion. Door, window and furniture are all fine wood carving artworks.

sense of richness and diversity.

The western part of the Humble Administrator's Garden is only half the size of the central part, and is also mainly an area of water scenery. The pond runs from north to south, and at the central part where the water widens there is also an islet built within. The surface of the water is shaped like a narrow carpenter's square. The main sceneries are concentrated at the northern part. At the north of the pond there is a Tower of Water Reflection, decorated with exquisitely-made long windows at the side facing the water and between columns. Through the windows scenes come to the eyes from their reflections on the water. You can catch the moon in the water, and see clouds floating on the pond surface, all from the glittering ripples. Opposite at the south of the pond is built the House of 36 Mandarin Ducks. If you push open the window and look outside in summer, you can see swaying lotuses in the pond and mandarin ducks playing in the water. A long corridor appears to delicately float on the water, reflecting the beauty of the division walls of central and western parts of the garden. The Liuting Pavilion looks like an abstract ship hull inside, and lotus fills the entire pond.

The Humble Administrator's Garden has a water area of three fifth of its entire area, and the majority of its architecture is built by the water. The Fragrant Islet Stone Bridge is beautifully shaped. Standing at the ship head, ripples reflect the light and brightness all around, reminding one of the old days when painted stone bridges were the rage. Rich vegetation is planted inside the garden in great variety, forming many scenic spots where plants and flowers are the

Rockery of Lion Forest Garden

Rockery of Lion Forest Garden is a most tortuous and complicated sample of Chinese classical garden rockeries. The garden, which was built at the end of the Yuan dynasty and the beginning of the Ming dynasty, utilized a great number of Huashigang relics belonged to the northern Song dynasty and intricate conception of rockery experts. The rockery group looked majestic and extensive. Since the rockeries were made of taihu lake stones distinguished for its characteristics of thin, wrinkled, leaked and penetrated, the rockeries were exquisite, delicate and full of caves. The rockery group composed a winding and bewildering maze. There were rock peaks and stalagmite on the rockeries, old trees, pines, cypresses grew on the gap and crevice. Kudzu vines and other creeping plants hung down from the stalamite, presenting vivid rustic charm. Divided into three levels of the top, middle and lower, the rockeries have 9 routes and 21 entrances. Along the winding rocky mountain paths, the tourist find himself sometimes at a peak, or a range, or a valley, or a cavity, sometimes entering a cave sometimes passing a bridge, sometimes high at the peak sometimes low at the cavity. He turns left or right, walks back and forth, quite an adventure he will enjoy.

The water scenic area in the middle part of the Humble Administrator's Garden, and the pond occupies three fifth of the garden's land area.

Xie

Platform for a *Xie* (a pavilion or a house on the terrace) in a Chinese garden is normally built upon the waterside, surrounded by low railings. The design for the roof is usually simple and poised, with flat and low eaves. A xie's main function is to appreciate views, but it can also be used as a place to relax for visitors.

theme and visual focus. In early spring, plum flowers at the Fragrant Snow and Clouds Pavilion blossom against the cold, and crabapple flowers at the Spring Crabapple Flower Dock weave a brocade of colors; in summer time at Jiashi Pavilion the loquat trees are laden with golden fruit; in autumn the fragrance of the rice flowers wafts into the Fragrant Sorghum Wind House; and in winter time pines and bamboos at the Pine Wind and Water Pavilion keep their green in the cold. The Tower of Viewing the Mountain feasts the eye, the Distant Fragrance Hall invigorates one's sense of smell, and the Rain Listening Hall pleases the ears with the sound of raindrops falling on banana leaves.

The current Humble Administrator's Garden, in comparison with the original one in the Zhengde Period of the Ming Dynasty, has more buildings and the islets added to it. Although the scenes somewhat lack the natural, open and lofty feel, the garden is still a masterpiece of meticulous work.

The Master-of-Nets Garden

In 1981, a permanent addition of artwork was put up in the Metropolitan Museum of Art in New York, and that is the classic Chinese garden Ming Xuan, the blue print of which is the Dian Chun Yi Garden in the Master-of-Nets Garden. The Master-of-Nets Garden is located in the Kuojiatou Alley at the south of Suzhou. The garden occupies a land area of only 0.4 hectare, less than one sixth of the Humble Administrator's Garden. But the garden is planned with meticulous care and precision, so that from the small we can see the grand. The many architectural forms do not clutter, and the small mountains and ponds do not seem cramped. The Master-of-Nets Garden is an outstanding example of "less is more" in classic Suzhou Gardens. Here primary scenes and secondary scenes complement each other in great variety, garden is built within garden, scene is made outside of scene, intricate designs exemplifying the ultimate in the art of garden

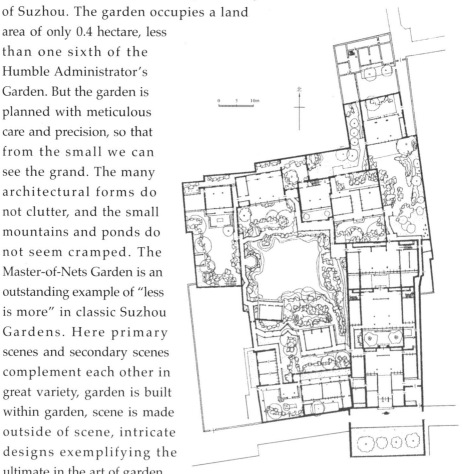

The ichnography of the Master-of-Nets Garden in Suzhou

building.

The Master-of-Nets Garden was first built in the Shaoxing Period (1131–1162) of the Southern Song Dynasty, after which ownership changed several times, until an official named Li took over and remodeled the garden to what it looks like today.

In the Master-of-Nets Garden, the residential area is located on the east whereas the garden area is located on the west. The architectural structures are numerous and dense in layout. The major scenic spot of the western garden area is a pond of merely 400 square meters in size, so one can imagine how hard it is to build a garden environment of superb design under such circumstances. In terms of the overall design of the entire garden, the east side of the garden is the residential area, divided into the inner residence and the outer residence. From the entrance to the garden through the residential gate, the halls are lined on the central axis in the order of the gate hall, the sedan hall, the main hall and the tower hall, all open and spacious in structure and tasteful in decoration. Courtyard clusters are formed with buildings utilizing artificial hills, corridors and windowed walls, which not only do not seem cramped, but rather give off a sense of tranquility and simple elegance. Located at north of the pond is the Pine-Watching and Reading Hall, with one artificial hill and two ancient pines closing into a courtyard. North of the Dianchunyi Garden at the northeastern side of the pond, lake stones dotted round and

Zhu Wai Yi Zhi Hall is a corridor house. Outside the gate and transparent window of the north wall is the green bamboo in front of the Jixu Study Room.

Xiexiu Storied Building serves as inner chambers, the furnishings of the hall pay attention to the function of practicality.

about, forming a bamboo and stone scene complemented with plum trees, bamboos and banana trees. Through the framed oblong windows, tall and straight bamboos fill the eye with green, and plum flowers blossom from artificial hills, as if in a classic Chinese painting. The architectural groups are each unique with their individual styles, independent yet interconnected with corridors and stone paths, avoiding the possible clutter of too many buildings.

The pond sits at the center of the western part of the garden. 20 meters long on the four sides and not large in total area, it is surrounded on all sides by buildings, which are meticulous in design and location. On the east side of the pond an octagonal-shaped Arriving Moon and Wind Pavilion protrudes over the bank, forming the major scene of the pond. On the western side the Duck Shooting Corridor connects with the walls of the residential area. Entering the pavilion from the residential area, you will be greeted with a refreshing scenery with pond under foot and the Arriving Moon and Wind Pavilion across the river; or looking across from the Arriving Moon and Wind Pavilion, you will face an entirely different scene. Lake stones and artificial hills sit below the Duck Shooting Corridor at half the height of the residential wall, hovering above the pond water, while the upper half of the residential walls are decorated with artificial windows. Pavilions with upturned eaves, stones and hills with rugged edges, artificial windows on the walls, bushes in between rocks and ancient pines in front of the pavilion together form a landscape painting at the east bank of the pond, against the background of residential walls. All these elements work together so successfully that no sense of monotony or disproportion is found with the high wall hovering over the water. At the north and south ends of the pond are found respectively the Pine Watching and Reading House and the Hills and Cassia House. As the houses are quite large in dimensions, care is taken that artificial hills are built before the houses so that they are half hidden behind the stones and the water. On the northwest and southeast end of the pond, small creeks and bays are built with stone bridges across them, forming the entry point and exit of the water, which thus immediately comes to life. The pond is surrounded with stones and rocks but built with only a few pavilions scattered here and there. Vegetation completes the scene of wilderness with hills and water. Through all this meticulous treatment, the not-so-large pond now stands apart from all the constructions around it.

In the late Qing Dynasty, the majority of garden owners were aristocrats and rich merchants, who had a high demand for comfort in their living quarters and a need for many types of architecture. However, if there were disproportionately large groups of architectural structures in the garden, the elegant simplicity held so dear by the men of intellect for generations would have to be sacrificed. Under the unfavorable condition of having too many buildings, the Master-of-Nets Garden has maintained the elegance and taste of the natural scene, serving as a positive example of gardens from that period.

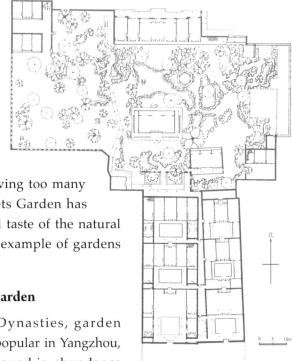

The ichnography of the Geyuan Garden in Yangzhou

The Geyuan Garden

In the Ming and Qing Dynasties, garden construction was extremely popular in Yangzhou, and private gardens were found in abundance both inside and outside the city. Frequent ravages of the war have left few gardens in full conservation, and one of them is the Geyuan Garden. The Geyuan Garden used to be the private residence of the rich salt merchant Huang Yingtai, and was built in the 23rd year of the Jiaqing Period, Qing Dynasty. Huang Yingtai was also named "Geyuan", and the garden was abundant with bamboo (written in Chinese characters as two of the ge characters side by side), and thus the name of the garden "Geyuan".

The Geyuan Garden is situated within Yangzhou city proper behind the Huang residence, and is 0.55 hectare in size. There is not much construction except for the "Seven-room Building" of two levels

Lou
Houses (*lou*) in a Chinese garden are mostly two or three-storied buildings functioned as bedrooms, studies or rooms with a view. The majority of them lie behind the hall in the gardens of the Ming dynasty. Due to its height, normally it itself would pose as a sight, which is especially true with a background of hills or lakes.

that overlook the entire garden, serving as the place for social activities of the owner. At the southeast end of the garden three halls named "Wind Chasing and Moonlight Filtering" are built, which were ideal for watching snow scenes in winter.

The most outstanding feature of this garden is the way the rocks are piled in the garden. On the west side of the "Seven-Room Building", a large artificial hill is built with lake stones, with the highest point at the center of the hill at 6 meters. Interspersed on both sides, the rocks go all the way down into the water. A stone room is built within the hill, with winding paths leading deep inside; and it is the coolest hideaway in summer. The entire body of the hill is built with lake stones, each curiously shaped, delicately textured, and grayish white in color, and the hill is named "Summer Hill". At the east end of the building, however, the hill is built with yellow stone, forming the main peak 7 meters in height with all kinds of peaks, ridges, and mountain ranges. Paths twist and turn within the hill, joining gullies, valleys and cave houses. On the west side of the hills, the setting sun paints the ochre-colored stone surface with the color of the golden fall, and thus the name "Autumn Hill" is given to the hill. The Wind Chasing and Moonlight Filtering Hall is built for the enjoyment of winter snow scenes, therefore pale white stones are placed in the shady area below the walls of the front hall, creating an illusion of unthawed snow. The hill is therefore named "Winter Hill". These three artificial hills, together with the "Spring Hill" built with stone shaped like bamboo-shoots, form the highlight of the Geyuan Garden with mountain scenes symbolizing spring, summer, autumn and winter. Although not large in size, the pond in the garden is built with twisting and turning banks, and small bays run into the caves of the Summer and Autumn Hills, which make the little pond suddenly come to life. The entire bank of the pond is built with lake stones, some of which touch upon the water surface while others hover above the water forming caves, adding further to the sense of agility of the pond water.

The Geyuan Garden was a private garden built during the Jiaqing Period (1796–1820) of the Qing Dynasty. Private gardens in the late Qing period, especially those owned by aristocrats and rich merchants, were keen on the pursuit of luxury and the show-off of riches, unlike the simple elegance and subtle style of Scholar gardens. The Geyuan Garden is a typical example of gardens of this period. Despite the beauty of the stones of four seasons, the garden's overly ornate artistry has taken away much of its natural appeal.

Shan Yi
Chinese traditional art was particular about being reserved and implicit. In this case, a rockery, named as *Shanyi (blocking the view with a rockery)*, was usually built to block the entrance of a garden so as to slowly lead visitors to a wonderland. Following labyrinth-like paths or circling around lakes, visitors will be enabled to see more and better sceneries step by step, gradually lost themselves in the spectacular views.

The entrance of the Geyuan Garden is a round-shape gate with bamboo planted outside.

Celebrated Gardens of the North

Construction of the Gardens

The northern region is quite different from the south in terms of natural conditions, economic development and culture. As the north is low in temperature in winter times, vegetation, due to the climate, is rarely evergreen. In winter, except for a few types of pines and cypresses, most trees and bushes have nothing left but bare branches. And even in spring and summer, there is not such a variety of trees and flowers as in the south. The northern economy, whether in agricultural production or in urban commerce and trading, was also not as developed as that of the south, and up until the Ming and Qing Dynasties, grains and daily supplies were mostly shipped from the south through the Grand Canal. However, most dynasties have set up their political center in the north, especially Beijing. As the capital city of the Yuan, Ming and Qing Dynasties, Beijing harbored a large number of members of the royalty and aristocrats, who had the political power and economic privilege to pursue pleasure, and a large number of gardens were thus built out of demand. The royalty and aristocracy are often artistically well educated. While amongst them there was no lack of garden builders who aspired to the traditional garden style of the literati, most opted for extravagance and luxury. Although many garden artisans were called in to the north to build gardens, but differences in natural conditions, political and cultural backgrounds as well as architectural styles had set the northern gardens apart from the gardens in the south.

In addition to gardens of the officials, rich merchants and the intellectuals, there is another type of private garden in Beijing, and that is the garden within the prince palaces. In the Qing Dynasty, the royalty were concentrated in the capital city. Palaces

Overlooking the Forbidden City from the Jing Shan Park.

for princes were thus residences given to the royalty. The royalty, with their family position, size and wealth, could certainly not be satisfied with a simple Siheyuan courtyard, and consequently a royal residence made up of multiple Siheyuan courtyards with both living quarters and gardens attached came into being in the capital city.

Private gardens in Beijing are mostly concentrated around the Shichahai Lake and in the northwest suburbs of Haidian.

During the Yuan Dynasty, in order to solve the problem of water shortage in the central districts of Beijing, the court had decreed to have water drawn into the city from Qinghe River and Jade Spring Hills northwest of Beijing, connecting the northwestern river system with the Shichahai Lake, the Tonghui River and the Grand Canal. This not only helped solve the water shortage problem in Beijing but also facilitated the transportation of supplies from the south. Therefore the Shichahai region became the bustling business center of Beijing. By the Ming and Qing Dynasties, of this region many private gardens appeared. The water level in Tonghui River dropped, and northern bound boats were only able to dock at the southern suburbs of Beijing. Shishahai lost its past bustling prosperity but remained a valuable water region where water is clear, lotuses and water-nuts fill the pond, and water fowls play and weave through the water plants in flocks. Within three or four li of this region many private gardens appeared.

The northwestern suburb of Beijing has the Shou'an Mountain Ranges headed by the fragrant hills at a distance, as well as the Jade Spring Hill and the Wongshan Mountain nearby. The most unique feature of this area is its rich water supply. The Jade Spring Hill is rich in spring water since ancient times, and in the plain area nearby water can easily be found without digging deeper than three feet. In front of the Wongshan Mountain the excess water pools into a lake, named Wongshan Pool in ancient times, and also known as the West Lake. The northwestern suburb, became a famous scenic area. As a result, the Ming Dynasty aristocrats, noblemen and scholars mostly chose to have their gardens built here, the most famous of which are the Qinghua Garden and the Ladle Garden.

The Qinghua Garden was a private garden of Ming royalty. It takes up 80 hectares of land space, and is located approximately at the east of the Summer Palace and south of the Yuanmingyuan Garden. The Ladle Garden was the private garden of a famous Ming Dynasty poet Mi Wanzhong, and was built in the Wanli Period (1573–1619) of the Ming Dynasty. It is located southeast of the Qinghua Garden, with water scenes as its main feature. The architecture is sparse and simple, following the classic garden style of the scholars.

In the Qing Dynasty many of the remaining Ming gardens were taken by the government and bestowed to the royalty, aristocrats and officials. These "bestowed" gardens are lined around the imperial gardens, forming a large garden area of the northwestern suburbs.

Famous Gardens of the North

The Prince Gong Palace Garden

The Prince Gong Palace Garden is also called "Garden of Gathered Brocade". It is the largest and the most well preserved garden among the dozens of gardens in Beijing, and is the only prince palace open to the public as a garden. The Prince Gong Palace Garden is ingeniously laid out with scenes that please the eye, and some even say that it is the prototype for the garden in the famous Chinese classic "The Dream of the Red Mansion".

The overall construction of the Prince Gong Palace can be divided into the residence area and the garden area, with the former in front and the latter in the back. The garden takes up 28 thousand square meters, and includes 31 historic buildings. The subsequent owner of the garden, the Gong Prince Yixin, summoned hundreds of the best craftsmen to reconstruct the garden, combining both the southern garden style and the northern architectural layout, and the western mingling with the Chinese architectural elements. The whole garden is laid out in 3 routes.

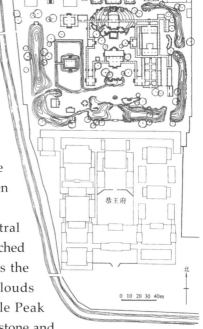

The ichnography of the Garden of Gathered Brocade in the prince Gong's Mansion

Entering the garden through the central gate, one can first see a Western style arched door of white marble. Facing the gate is the 5-meter-high Dule Peak, shaped like clouds rolling back and forth. Behind the Dule Peak there is Anshan Hall, sitting on a base of stone and connected with the eastern and western wing rooms by corridors to form a three-sided courtyard opening

The Yishu Garden where various vegetables were planted to seek for the wild interest in the Cuijin Garden

to the south.

In Qing Dynasty Beijing, channeling running water into a private residence would need the emperor's consent, an honor rarely bestowed except for a few prince palaces, and the Prince Gong Palace is one of them. Within the garden there is a large bat-shaped pond built with green stone named the "Bat Pond". Elm trees encircle the pond, and in the season when the elm seeds fall, the coin-shaped seeds cover the Bat Pond, implying "wealth and fortune (bat is homonymous with fortune in Chinese)". Crossing the hall to enter the central courtyard, one can find a stone hill called "Rock of Dripping Green", the major scene of the entire garden. In front of the hill there is a small pond, and behind the pond there is a cave called "Cave of Secret Cloud", inside which there is a stone tablet with the word "fortune" personally inscribed by Emperor Qianlong. At the north of the Rock of Dripping Green is the Bat Hall, a hall shaped like a bat. Main constructions such as the garden gate, the Anshan Hall, the Rock of Dripping Green and the Bat Hall are all located at the

The gate of the east line of the Garden of Gathered Brocade

central axis of the Prince Gong Palace residential area, forming a standardized central part.

The east route of the Garden of Gathered Brocade is made up of dense architectural groups. The southern part is composed of two parallel-running long and narrow Siheyuan Courtgards, The northern part is the grand opera stage, a large architectural structure including the front hall, the grand hall for watching the opera, the stage and the backstage. On the eastern route and in the courtyard with decorated doors, the most elegant architecture is the "Refreshing Autumn Pavilion" or the "Running Wine Cup Pavilion", built with a twisting and turning creek 10 centimeters wide shaped like the Chinese character "pavilion". It is an ideal setting for scholars to get together.

There is very little architecture on the western route. This area is mostly made up of mountain scenery and water scenery. Scattered within the garden are the Lake-center Pavilion, Cloud Washing Residence and Firewood Fragrance Path. Within the Lakecenter Pavilion there are three water pavilions, which are named "Stone Boat of Poetry and Paintings". Gazing at the green ripples, a small boat sitting idly by the lakeside and the reflection of mountains and trees in the waters is enough to take away all worldly cares.

The Garden of Gathered Brocade, being a prince palace, has a larger number of architecture and a more formally laid-out courtyard compared with private gardens of scholars. It not only has the grand halls and lobbies rarely seem in scholar's private gardens, but also the grand opera stage hardly found in private gardens of government officials. But it is, after all, a garden of the prince palace, where the garden builder uses many techniques to differentiate the garden area from the residential area. First of all, care is taken that the overall environment is well planned. For example, at the entry way through the garden gate, artificial hills are built on both sides with green stone, and flowers and trees are planted on the hills. Paths on the hills extend to the east and the west, passing through hill after hill, creating a mood of the wild mountains and woods. In addition, hills made of earth are built on the external sides of the eastern and western route, closing off the outside bustle to form a complete garden environment. Secondly, local treatment of mountain and woods is emphasized. Within the more formally laid-out courtyards on the central and eastern route, irregular-shaped ponds, mountains and rocks are used in addition to the lush bamboo, ancient pines, ancient Chinese locusts and other trees and bushes and flowers to break the rigid and stale air of the formally-planned architecture. Last of all, the western route is designed as an area of natural scenery, with water and hills as the main body. The relaxed and simple layout brings a refreshing air to the entire garden. The Prince Gong Palace Garden is therefore a garden with royal grandeur but not lacking in natural beauty.

Xichunyuan Garden

The Xichunyuan Garden lies to the east of the Garden of Splendor in Haidian, which is in the Qinghua Campus today. The garden was originally built in the Kangxi Period (1662–1722), and in the Daoguang Years (1821–1850) it was bestowed to the two royal princes to live in. The Xichunyuan Garden is divided into two parts of east and west, the east being called the "Qinghua Garden" and the west "Jinchun Garden".

Both Jinchun Garden and Qinghua Garden are built on the flatland, and they utilize the readily available underground water supply to dig ponds and make artificial hills with earth. But they are not quite the same either in planning or scenery design. In Jinchun Garden was dug a ring-shaped pond with a small island in the center. The buildings of the garden are concentrated on this island. Earth left from digging the pond is utilized to make hills around the pond, and the ring-shaped pond and ring of hills surround the group of buildings in the center. Although circular in shape, the pond has both narrow and wide water surface

The serene and refined interior scenery of courtyard in the Qinghua Garden

The water scenery of the Jin Chun Garden where embankment was built with yellow stone.

Yellow Stone

Yellow stone is made of yellowish brown or reddish brown quartz rock, sandstone, grit rock, moved and scoured by mountain torrents or river water. With a smooth surface and an arresting yellowish brown color, it reflects greasy or waxy gloss, bringing a delightful sensation of comfort and tenderness. Since yellow stone is mainly made up of silica, it is very hard and solid in texture, cracks, holes or cavities are rarely seen, which makes the difference between *yellow* stone and taihu lake stone.

areas and irregular-shaped banks, where docks of yellow stone are built. With lotus planted in the water, and willows and Chinese locusts around the water, an open landscape effect is achieved. The layout of Qinghua Garden is different in that the residence area sits in front and the garden area is in back. The residence area comprises an orderly architectural group. Entry through the gate leads through the hall to the I-shaped lobby in the back, forming the front and the back courtyards from south to north, connected by corridors on all sides. On the east and west sides of this central axis two courtyard groups stand side by side, weaving in corridors and circular or bottle-shaped doors. Within these courtyards evergreens like pine and cypress are planted together with flowering trees of crabapples, pears and magnolia. Artificial hills are built in the central backyard, and the yard gives no sense of being shut in

The waterside corridor pavilion in the Jin Chun Garden

but rather a delightful taste of a garden scene. Closely linked to this group of architecture is a large pond with crooked banks and yellow stone docks, as well as trees all around. On the east bank of the pond there is a small pavilion, where as the south bank is an I-shaped platform extending into the water for the enjoyment of the water scene. Although the garden area is not large in size, the secluded environment and all the hills and water nearby are rich in the charms of nature, thus the name "Qinghua of water and woods".

In 1860, the allied troops of the British and the French army invaded Beijing, and burnt the Garden of Perfect Splendor to the ground. In the Tongzhi Period (1862–1874) of the Qing Dynasty, the court decided to demolish all the nearby gardens so as to pool the materials for the reconstruction of the Garden of Perfect Splendor. All the architecture in Xichun Garden was destroyed. The architecture of Jinchun Garden, which is west of the Garden of Perfect Splendor, was also completely destroyed. Fortunately the Qinghua Garden on the east side remained intact, but the garden had fallen into disuse and gradually became deserted. In 1909, in order to set up the preparatory school for overseas students to the US, the Qing government rediscovered the site of the Xichun Garden, and decided to set up a school in Qinghua Garden with its large land area and remnant architecture. The school was named the "Qinghua School", which is the predecessor of the Qinghua University today. For nearly one hundred years, constructions in the Qinghua Garden had been repeatedly renovated, but the base of the architecture and the overall layout had never been altered. Even the two ancient cypress trees and the rocks are things from the past. Today taking a stroll on the campus of Qinghua University you can see all the architecture brought back to its original Qing style, and the classic look of the garden restored. Although all constructions in the Jinchun Garden were destroyed, the lakes and hills remain. In 1927, the famous writer Zhu Ziqing who taught at Qinghua University wrote the famous prose "Moonlight on Lotus Pond". The work was written when he was taking a stroll around the lake after reading in the heat of a summer night. It is no doubt that the garden environment and the mood it evokes transcends all times.

Construction Techniques of Private Gardens

Private gardens, regardless whether from the north or the south, whether built by scholars, officials, aristocrats or rich merchants, all have one thing in common—they all try to re-create an environment close to nature in an area with limited space. Looking through the building practices of classic private gardens, we can derive the following experiences and techniques which have become the guiding principles and rules and passed down from generation to generation.

The Grand View Garden (partial) painted by Qing painter based on the Chinese classic novel *The Dream of Red Mansion*. The painting shows the flourishing sceneinnoble families.

Flexibility in overall Layout

Classic Chinese architecture, if looked at individually, is mostly simple in shape and not large in volume. However they often appear in groups, which is one of the differing features from Western architecture. Judging from documentation from ancient times and the remaining examples, we can conclude that this kind of architectural combination had adopted the courtyard model from very early on, which is to form a courtyard with single buildings on all sides. The main building sits in the center, flanked by the secondary buildings on either side, forming a layout with a central axis. However, garden construction breaks this rule, and in order to create in a limited space an environment that emulates nature, a flexible and overall layout is creatively adopted.

Like all other kinds of architecture, architecture in gardens has to fulfill its functional demand. In private gardens, the owner has multiple needs for daily living, reading, entertaining and enjoyment, and architecture must fulfill each of these demands— the residence to be secluded, reading area to be quiet, entertaining section to be convenient and the area for enjoyment to embody the mood of nature and the natural landscape—all these elements are concerns when planning the garden. In addition, the garden must possess beauty, a beautiful environment that can measure up to any found in nature.

The layout of the architecture has to both "make scenery" and to "get scenery", which means that the position and image of the architecture must form an enjoyable view within the garden, and at the same time from within the architecture one must be able to enjoy one scene or multiple scenes in the garden. In Jichang Garden in Wuxi, the Fish Watching Fence at the eastern bank of the pond's mid section is the main scenic spot of the pond area, and at the same time standing at the fence the entire mountain

The furnishings inside the buildings and the scenery in garden echo each other at a distance.

The East lake in Shaoxing—buildings, bridges and natural sceneries harmonize with each other.

view on the western side of the garden greets the eye. The Jiashu Hall at the northwestern corner of the garden is the main view at the top of the entire garden, and at the mean time from inside the hall one can overlook the water scene of the entire garden, and also see from a distance the mountains and Buddhist pagoda outside the garden.

Architecture in a garden environment does not exist in isolation, but rather forms a comprehensive scene together with the nearby mountains, waters and vegetation. In the Humble Administrator's Garden, the Fragrant Snow and Clouds Pavilion is not an isolated pavilion—it sits on the islet mountain at the center of the pond, set off by flowers and plants on all sides, supported by rock hills from the bottom and surrounded by a pond full of lotus flowers in summer time. At the east bank of the pond in the Master-of-Nets Garden, the Duck Shooting Corridor, the rock hills on its south and the year round colorful vegetation beside the corridor and among the rocks and stones form a colorful painting against the backdrop of white-washed walls. Hills, water and architecture form scenic spots, and multiple scenic spots form scenic areas. Scenic spots and scenic areas work in synergy to create a garden with more beauty than the eye can take in.

The classic Chinese garden must be at the same time seeable, tour-able and livable, whereby all scenic spots and areas must be connected by paths for convenience of getting around. In order to create constantly-changing scenes along the way, twisted paths are suitable while straight roads are forbidden. Paths in open air coexist with corridor paths that shield from the sun and rain. Some of the paths are built along the wall, some are twisting and turning, some move up and down over the slope of the hills, while still others hover above water into water corridor or covered bridges. Along these winding paths and corridors, the builder meticulously sets up a variety of scenes, either a hall, a pavilion, or water pavilion, or an ancient tree, banana trees or a cluster of bamboos. Even a pile of rocks, when placed on hilltops, by the pond, or at the end of the road, can always add to the scene when reasonably and cleverly positioned. Moving along the path, the tourist will be refreshed by the ever-changing scenes, scenes that never tire the eye.

In order to expand the touring area in a not-so-large space, private gardens are often segmented into different scenic areas by corridors and walls. These walls are not high, and in addition to doorways there are often see-through windows on the walls, so that the walls divide but do not separate. These corridors and walls add to the scenes themselves, and they keep the scenic areas both connected and divided. In a larger garden, the garden builder must design at least one optimum route to tour around. Starting from the entry of the garden, one strolls on this route along stone paths or the bank of the pond, or enters a doorway, or climbs the mountain paths, or enters a hall, or takes a short rest in the water pavilion. Each move from one area to the next brings renewed scenes, extending the time and expanding the space for enjoyment.

The Lingering garden of Suzhou is a private garden relatively large in space. Its main entrance is located in between buildings on both sides and is only 8 meters in width. However the road leading to the garden area is as long as 40 meters. In this narrow area the garden builder arranged three spaces connected by winding corridors. Upon entry into the garden there is a small sky-light yard, and only by passing through the yard through the winding corridor does one get to see the second space with flowers and plants. Passing through another corridor the third space is reached, where an ancient tree leans against the wall, and only then does the mini hall connected to the corridor, and lined with lattice windows appear. Through the windows the main body of the garden can be seen. In here, halls, corridors and walls form a variety of

The Winding corridor not only is a scenic sight abounding in change of lines, but also creates a visual-viewing rhythm for a not so large garden space.

The stone path in the artificial mountainous scene

spaces, and the alternation in these spaces, the change from the ancient tree, and the flowers and plants, bring varied and ever-changing pleasure to the viewer.

Imitation of Natural Mountains and Waters

The stone cave built with natural hollowed-out lake stones.

The ancient Chinese gardens and parks of earlier periods were enclosure gardens formed with real mountains and waters. Ever since the Wei, the Jin and the South and North Dynasties, the practice of simulating natural mountains and waters came into being. In the Song Dynasty, an imperial garden called Gen Yue was built in the eastern capital of Bianliang, and the Huizong Emperor (period of reign 1101–1125) demanded that the magnificence of

The waterside small hill piled with yellow stone and earth

The pond connects the inner structures with outdoor sceneries skillfully

the Five Mounts in China be represented and the precipitous Sichuan mountain paths reproduced, leading the craft of creating artificial mountains and waters to its peak. By the Ming and Qing Dynasties, imitating nature had already become an important craft in garden construction among private gardens.

First let us look at the making of mountains. From appearance, natural mountains are often high and low in their rolling hills, and there are always the main peak and the subsidiary peaks. The hillsides are often covered with lush vegetation. As to build mountains in the garden it is most undesirable for mountain peaks to lie side by side or to have several peaks lined up like a paintbrush stand. The way peaks are organized depends on the requirement of the scenes. Whether the scene is to be open and spacious or deep and quiet determines the number, the size and the arrangement in height of the peaks. Mountains are built using earth, stone or both. Built with lake stones, the mountain looks delicate and lively. Built with yellow stones, the mountain looks natural and majestic. Mountains of earth should be covered with flowers and plants for a lush appearance, and stones should be scattered among the earth as if they appear out of the ground. Stone mountains should also be filled with earth

The lattice window at the entrance of the Lingering Garden

in between rocks, and flowers and plants should be planted in there for a natural lively look. Within natural mountains there should be no lack of gullies, mountain paths and stone caves, and artificial mountains should follow this rule as well.

Now let us look at the management of water. Private gardens are often built within the city, and for this reason even in the south where water abounds, most garden ponds are dug by men. In nature the everflowing rivers twist and turn, the lakes and ponds extend into the distance, and for this reason artificial

The irregular embankment etherealizes the not so large water scene

ponds should never be regular and square in shape, but need to be crooked and natural. Where there is a large water surface, small bridges should be placed to break up the pond into large and small water areas for a gradation of the water scene. The end of the pond often turns into a small bay, stopping at the corner of the house or underneath the water pavilion,

The flying eaves and warped cornus of the Rain Wrapping Building in Yu Garden, Shanghai.

where the water seems to disappear. A pond of still water is thus brought to life. Water plants should be planted to create a sense of liveliness to the water but not to fill up the entire water space, because they should not block the shadow of buildings in the water. It is appropriate to place yellow stones or lake stones along twining banks of the pond. Stones are placed at different heights. Standing on the high points one can see the scenery on all four sides, whereas standing on the low points one can easily play with the water.

In a natural environment it is common for mountains and waters to coexist. But when there is a cave in the mountain and endlessly-flowing water in the cave, it is then considered a scene of wonders. And the private gardens venture to imitate the scene. The Summer Hill of the Yangzhou Geyuan Garden is built by the pond, with stone caves winding deep into the hill. Water from the pond twists into the cave, bringing a sense of coolness and adding a new dimension to the name Summer Hill.

Mountains and water can be regarded as the soul of the natural environment gardens. Mountain adds spirit and water adds liveliness to the scenery. It is only through a profound understanding of the natural mountains and waters that one can accurately condense and extract their real essence, and represent them faithfully in the construction of gardens.

Meticulous Attention to Treatment of Details

Private gardens cannot afford the vast space of imperial gardens, or the imposing groups of architecture. Instead their space is complex and contained, including a full array of architectural types, mountains, waters and vegetation. Therefore to create a place fit for seeing, touring and living, in addition to efforts made in the general layout, great attention must be paid to the treatment of details in the architecture, the mountains, the waters and the vegetation.

First let us look at the architecture. There are many kinds of

The waterside pavilion is connected by the outer corridor.

architecture within the private garden. To take the pavilion as an example, there are pavilions that are square, oblong, circular, pentagonal, hexagonal, octagonal, plum flower-shaped, cross-shaped, fan-shaped, double squared and double circular, each placed in its appropriate location within the garden, some already a scene in itself while still others a perfect

The spacious round gate in the garden wall has the function of view framing.

spot for the enjoyment of the scenery. On the Blowing Platform on the Slender West Lake in Yangzhou is a square pavilion that is an important scenic spot on the lake. There are walls built of earth on all four sides of the pavilion, and on each wall there is a circular doorway carved out. Looking out from one of the doorways is the scene of Five Pavilion Bridge on the lake, and from another doorway the Lama Pagoda can be seen from afar. The doorways frame the lake scenes into perfect pictures. Most gardens of the scholars and most private gardens in the south have maintained a similar style in decorum, despite the variety of halls, houses, and buildings—there is never the use of the five-colored antique roof tiles, the use of colorful paintings on roof beams and frames, nor painting window and door frames in red and gold. Instead the use of black-colored flat tiles, brown roof beams, white-washed walls and gray bricks tightly knit the architecture with the mountains, waters and vegetation in an elegant manner.

Doorways on houses and courtyard walls are often oblong, circular, octagonal, plumflower-shaped, flower, ruyi-shaped or various kinds of bottle-shaped. In addition to the commonly-shaped windows, there are patterned glass windows, lattice windows and empty windows with nothing but frames. Just in Suzhou gardens alone there are hundreds of styles of window lattice patterns and empty window shapes. These different windows look like flowers painted on a white sheet of paper from a distance, but only when looked at from up close does one see the meticulous and handsome craftsmanship. The window frames are often pieced together carefully with gray bricks, finely polished and lined with different borders. Whether geometrical or foliage shaped, the lattice pattrns are all molded with brick strips and clay, giving a clean outline and sharp image. This kind of fine artwork that reflects the high skills of the southern craftsmen has become the exemplary stroke of genius for the private gardens within this region.

On the gate facing the grand hall and the gate of the Xiexiu Mansion courtyard wall at the Master-of-Nets Garden, there is a

decorative doorhead attached to the wall that imitates wooden structure with bricks. One of the doorheads has on both sides of the beam carved stage scenes complete with figures and buildings, and the multilayered carving was done so meticulously that even the facial expressions of the figures are clearly visible. On the sides of the other doorhead there are also carved images of chimes (qing-homonymous with "celebrate") and fish (yu-homonymous with "abundance"), meaning auspicious happiness with overabundance.

Grounds in the gardens are often paved with bricks, pebbles, stone

Zao Yao Gao Xiang doorhead built by bricks in the Master of Nets Garden.

An elegant and quiet courtyard with study room and primitively simple paving in South China gardens.

pieces or bricks. Craftsmen like to use their varying styles, colors and textures to make patterns on the floor, mostly geometrical or foliage-shaped and sometimes even in the shape of animals such as lions or deer. After being washed a few times by the spring rain, fresh green sprouts push through the stone gaps on the road surfaces with different patterns, adding to its freshness and life.

In nature, plants vary by region. In addition to utilizing the existing trees and vegetation, the garden builder would carefully choose the most appropriate types of plants and trees. Through observation and research on the growth of trees, flowers and plants, and by the way they grow, the way they look, their growth period, as well as the color of their flowers and foliage, the garden builder would determine what combination of plants to use, and match the plants to fulfill the need of the garden environment.

In northern courtyard gardens choices are mainly focused

on trees that blossom in spring, provide shade in summer and bear fruit in autumn. Commonly found trees include pears, crabapples, pomegranates, jujubes, persimmons and grapes.

Gardens in the south have, of course, a much greater number of choices in terms of plants. Peach blossoms and willows greet the spring, and in most cases they are planted in rows. In the early spring, willows come out with the first sprouts, a mist of green when looked at from afar. In addition, maple trees are often used to dye the deep autumn, whereas pines and cypresses, which are green all year round, tall and straight, are even more magnificent when covered with snow in winter. Banana trees and bamboos are green in all seasons in the south, which are the most commonly-found greenery in the gardens. Ancient garden builders often used the ophiopogon japonicus to mask imperfections of artificial mountains, because their long leaves are elegant like the orchid plant, simple, tender, reserved and poised and have come to symbolize the character of the Chinese people.

Although these plants and trees already have a wide array of shapes and forms, they still need further pruning and cutting to suit the requirement of the gardens. The branches, leaves and crowns of trees are all carefully pruned not only to enhance their original beauty but also to work in harmony with surrounding architecture, rocks and ponds for the utmost visual effect. Even water plants used to decorate the water surface are carefully selected and matched. Lotus flowers, although beautiful, need to be planted in jars before being selectively planted under water, so that they only blossom in selected areas. On larger water surfaces,

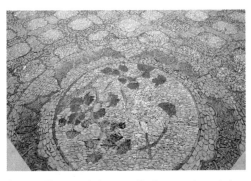

Ground with crane design paved by the grey stones looks elegant.

Pot chrysanthemum in the halls of garden

Naturally-created abstract sculptures—
Tai Lake Stone Peak in Chinese garden.

Taihu Stone

Formed on dongting west mountain by the taihu lake in Jiangsu province and other small islands, Taihu lake stone, is made of limestone shaped by chemical deposition. Numerous limestone inundated in small waves has long been undergone waves' abrasive mechanical wear and chemical erosion. As a result, either a hole or cavity is formed on the limestone after piercing through, or otherwise a vortex is formed without being pierced through. Therefore, those stones are normally round and smooth, delicate and cool, covered with lines and cavities connected to each other. Their shapes are usually bizarre and fantastic. Four words are used to describe the odd feature of taihu lake stone: thin, wrinkled, leaked and penetrated.

it is often the practice to plant lotus at a distance and water lilies nearby and under the bridge, because water lily leaves are more tiny and delicate, suitable to look at from close up.

Many scenes in gardens are created from the inspiration of plants. On the southeastern and southwestern corners of the Humble Administrator's Garden, there are two courtyards with halls, respectively named "Loquat Garden" and "Magnolia Hall" after the trees planted in there. In the Lingering Garden of Suzhou, there is an ancient tree leaning against the corner of the wall with withered trunk and branches. The weathered form of the tree against the whitewashed wall makes up a scene of ancient wood with crisscrossed branches.

In addition to flowers and plants planted in the ground, bonsais and potted plants with different flowering seasons are also used to decorate the garden. In front windowsills or under the steps of halls, around pavilions, upon rocks by water banks there are often scattered potted plants to add a finishing touch to a simple and elegant environment. Within the halls, against a stark background of black pillars, whitewashed walls and dark wood furniture, a few pots of autumn chrysanthemums immediately bring life and color to the entire room.

The making of natural scenery gardens would not be complete without stones and rocks. In addition to making mountains, building houses, paving roads, building bridges or laying water banks out of rocks, people of ancient times liked to create scenes with a single rock or a pile of rocks. In private gardens, scenes created with stones and rocks can be found everywhere, in front of and behind houses, under corridors and by the corner of walls, one can often find a single-stone scene or a multiple stones scene. The desired form of the stone should appear slender, pierced, carved, and empty within. Scenes made from these stones can match a work of art carved out by nature. Sometimes plants and flowers are placed beside or below the stones, further enhancing the beauty of the garden scene.

In private gardens of the Ming and Qing Dynasties, it is common practice to construct scenes with a single rock or stone. In the Hall of the Five Peak Fairies in the eastern region of the Lingering Garden in Suzhou, stone peaks rise from among the lush bamboos, symbolizing the famous Five Mounts of China. In the Garden of Gathered Brocade in the Beijing Prince Gong Palace Garden, there is a "Flying-in Stone" that serves both as a protective screen at the entry and the first scene that meets the eye upon entering the garden.

The Five Pavilion Bridge in the Slender West Lake in Yangzhou.

Magnificent Imperial Gardens

Following the decision to move the capital from Nanjing to Beijing in 1403, the Ming emperor started to rebuild the city based on the layout of the Grand Capital of the previous Yuan Dynasty. The sparsely populated northern district of the city was demolished, and the south city wall was stretched further south, which expanded the front border of the Imperial City. Palaces had to be rebuilt as the palatial buildings of the Yuan Dynasty were severely damaged in the flames of wars. Unlike the usual practice of burning down the palaces of previous dynasties, the rulers of the Qing Dynasty continued to use the whole palatial architectural groups of the Ming Forbidden City without making major changes. With Beijing as the center, the Chinese ancient imperial gardens that we can still visit today were mainly built in the Ming and Qing Dynasties.

The designers and the gardeners of imperial gardens in the Ming and Qing Dynasties extensively absorbed the building experience of private gardens from previous dynasties, and combined the essences of building techniques of gardens of all times and from all over the world. Some even directly imitated the layout or rebuilt at the original site of private gardens. Imperial gardens are interspersed with surrounding magnificent palaces, evoking a majestic splendor. Imperial resorts or temporary imperial residences beautifully recreate the tranquility and simplicity of the natural landscape in limited space by playing upon natural hills and waters, or making man-made hills or lakes. The Waiba Temples (The Eight Outer Temples) in the Mountainous Summer Resort in Chengde well reflect the religious features of the monastic gardens in the Ming and the Qing Dynasties. Deeply enchanted by the scenic beauty of the West Lake, Emperor Qianlong ordered the imitation of some natural scenes of the West Lake, such as "Dancing Lotus in Summer Wind in Courtyard" and "Autumn Moon Reflected in Peaceful Lake" to be built in the Garden of Perfect Splendor.

As symbols of royal power, imperial gardens are incredibly magnificent and splendid. Looking up at the Longevity Hill from the Yun Hui Yu Yu Decorated Archway near the bank of the Kunming Lake, one can see that the Dispelling Cloud Gate, the Dispelling Cloud Hall, the Moral Excellence Hall and the Tower of Buddhist Incense are vertically distributed on the hillside along a north-south axis. Signifying the power of God, the Tower of Buddhist Incense lies at the top of the hill with a height of 41 meters, overlooking everything down below. Designed as the center and the landmark of the whole garden planning, the Dispelling Cloud Hall is located at the middle of the axis. The whole architectural complex fully exemplifies the Chinese concept of heaven and also reflects the feudalistic ideology that helped to maintain the autarchy of emperors.

General Introduction of Imperial Gardens of the Ming and Qing Dynasties

Imperial gardens of the Ming Dynasty were mainly built inside the Imperial City and the Forbidden City. Inside the high walls of the Forbidden City, there lie the Imperial Garden at the north end of the axis and the Garden of Creating Happiness Palace at the northeast. Within the range of the Imperial City, the Longevity Hill stands to the north of the Forbidden City, while the Rabbit Garden and the West Gardens scatter in the west, the East Gardens in the southeast. Among all these gardens, the West Gardens are considered as the most important.

With a location close to the west of the Forbidden City, exploitations of the West Gardens can be dated back to early years. As early as 1151, the Jin kingdom that was founded by the Northern Nuzhen Minority set up its capital in Yanqing area, and named it the Middle Capital. Located in the northwest outskirts of the capital, the site of the West Gardens was originally an area of lake marsh that connected to the Gaoliang River. Taking advantage of the excellent natural environment, the rulers of the Jin built the Great Tranquility Palace as their imperial resort by transforming the marsh into a lake and making a man-made islet. This islet in the lake was named the Jade Flower Islet. The Guang Han Hall (Severe Coldness Hall) and huge rockeries were built afterwards.

In the 13th century, the Mongolian-founded Yuan Dynasty unified the separate kingdoms into one China. In 1272, the Yuan rulers decided to build their capital at the former site of the Middle Capital of the Jin. Though most buildings were severely damaged, the Great Tranquility Palace was still well preserved, therefore the Yuan emperor began to plan and build the new national capital—the Grand Capital—with the Great Tranquility Palace as the center of the city planning. The Great Tranquility Palace was walled inside

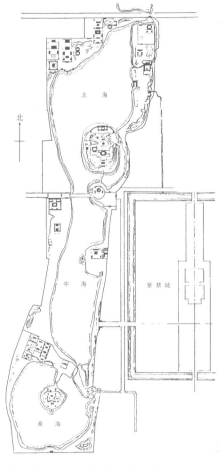

The ichnography of the Forbidden City and West Garden

the Imperial City and the lake was redesigned and renovated. Renamed as the Tai Ye Pond, the lake was located to the west of the Forbidden City inside the Imperial City layout. Imperial water resources in the northwest outskirts of the Grand Capital flowed into the lake through the Jin River. Large numbers of trees and shrubs were planted along the banks of the pond, and two more islets, the Yuan Di Islet and the Screen Mountain Islet, were formed. The former Jade Flower Islet was renamed the Longevity

Hill. With painstaking efforts and elaborate design, the Tai Ye Pond was transformed into an imperial garden full of the charm and appeal of nature inside the Imperial City.

In 1422, following the moving of the capital to Beijing, the rulers of the Ming Dynasty settled in the newly-built Forbidden City. The spatial relationship between the Forbidden City and the Tai Ye Pond was not changed, but large scale renovation was undertaken for the Tai Ye Pond. More buildings were constructed at the north bank and man-made landscapes were added without losing the natural beauty of the Tai Ye Pond. Along the east bank of the Yuan Di Islet, earth was piled so that the islet was changed into a "peninsula" that stretched to the east. Walls were built surrounding the earth platform and this newly-formed place was named the "Round City". The Tai Ye Pond was enlarged further down south resulting in a large increase of the size of water surface. The newly formed water body was called the South Sea and the water on the north of the Round City was

Overlooking the Round City and the Middle and South Sea from the North Sea Lake.

named the North Sea. Water between these two "seas" was called the Middle Sea. A new layout with the North, the Middle and the South Sea was formed on the site of former Tai Ye Pond. Since then, the West Gardens had become the most important imperial gardens inside the Ming Imperial City.

After the Qing military troops crossed the Great Wall borderline and entered into Beijing City, their rulers took the Forbidden City as their dwelling place. Original imperial gardens inside the Forbidden City were kept, and structures scattered in gardens around the three seas (the North, Middle and South Sea) were built, rebuilt or enlarged. Examples were the White Pagoda, several Buddhist buildings on the north bank of the North Sea, the Jing Qing Meditating Room inside the north yard, the natural scenery area and several architectural groups along the east bank of the North Sea, the Ying Platform in the South Sea and the Qin Zheng Hall on the north bank of the South Sea. With these new constructions, both the type and the number of architecture at structures were increased inside the West Gardens. The strengthening of cultural flavor in the gardens displays the typical style of imperial gardens—magnificent, luxurious and splendid. This kind of scale, style and feature was maintained for long time afterwards. The Middle and South Sea Garden is now where the Chinese central government is located, and the North Sea Garden is open to the public as a park. Today, these gardens are still the models and examples of planting and afforesting in Beijing City.

In 1994, the Mountainous Summer Resort in Chengde and the surrounding temples as a whole was added to the list of World Heritage by UNESCO for its unique architectural charm and achievements. Absorbing the essence of architectural art from both the north and the south, the resort stands as a perfect architectural example, which borrows the style, frame and building skills of southern style gardens while maintaining the

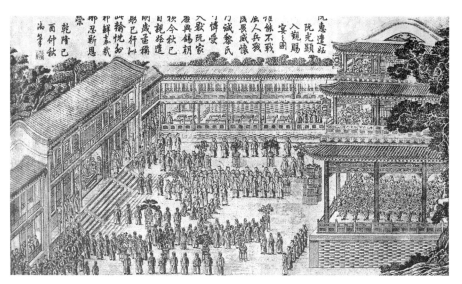

A painting of opera watching in the Summer Resort in Chengde in Qian Long years of the Qing Dynasty

common techniques used in garden building practice in the north.

In the 16th year of Emperor Kangxi's reign (1678), the Qing rulers started the regular inspection tours to the Outer Fortress (places north of the Great Wall) and the military training. These activities that usually took place in autumn gradually became traditions of the Qing Dynasty. Because of the pleasant climate in the Kalaqin herding areas in Mongolia, formal imperial pleasure grounds were gradually formed. Along the way from Beijing to those pleasure grounds, resorts and villas were built, the largest of those being the Summer Resort in Chengde. Originally a herding ground for Mongolians, this place is sparsely populated and boasts of rolling mountains covered with rich vegetation, plenty of underground springs and delightful weather. Being fond of this perfect environment, Emperor Qianlong ordered the Summer Resort to be built at the site. One large imperial garden began to take shape in the early years of the Qing Dynasty.

In 1735, the fourth emperor of the Qing Dynasty—Emperor Qianlong—ascended the throne and under his reign, China once again enjoyed a period of economic prosperity. Emperor Qianlong, who had a deep understanding of Han culture, was deeply impressed by the mountains, rivers and famous gardens that he visited during his six inspection tours to Southern China. Supervised by Qianlong himself, the construction of imperial gardens that started from Emperor Kangxi boomed in this period, which formed some clear-cut features: the excessive pursuit of artistic techniques made the gardens in this period overly polished and ornate.

Emperor Qianlong spent most of his efforts on the construction of imperial gardens in the northwest suburbs of Beijing and the

The design and construction of lakes area in the Summer Resort in Chengde were based on natural mountains and water

Mountainous Summer Resort in Chengde. Starting from 1751, it took 40 years to expand the Summer Resort. Scores of scenic spots were completed and eight Buddhist temples were built. These temples are known as "The Eight Outer Temples" at present. The Mountainous Summer Resort in Chengde became the largest and most magnificent imperial garden of that time.

The Garden Zone in the Northwest Outskirts of Beijing

Most of the Ming private gardens in the northwest outskirts of Beijing were left in a deserted state after the chaos caused by the war at the end of the Ming Dynasty. The Qing rulers then started a large-scale garden construction project. The former gardens, such as those in the Fragrant Hills and the Jade Spring Hill in the natural garden scenic district, were renovated and expanded. Some Ming private gardens were taken over and transformed into imperial gardens. The northwest outskirts of Beijing hence became a zone concentrating large numbers of gardens.

A small part of the West Mountain Range, the Fragrant Hills, is covered with lush trees and its climate is pleasant. As early as the period of the Liao (907–1125), Jin and Yuan Dynasties, there were temples built here and emperors paid visits now and then. In 1677, Kangxi reconstructed the temples in the Fragrant Hills and changed them into an imperial resort. In the period of Yongzheng and Qianlong's reign, this resort was expanded twice, and named the Jing Yi Garden in 1747.

A small hill rising out of the plain of the northwest suburbs, the Jade Spring Hill boasts of the abundance of spring water and deep forests. Several temples were built in the Jin and Yuan period. Under the reign of Kangxi, the emperor built the Cheng Xin Garden and later renamed the Jing Ming Garden. Later Qianlong enclosed parts of the river, lake and land nearby into the garden, and expanded the range of the Jing Ming Garden.

The construction of imperial gardens in the northwest outskirts of the Qing Dynasty began in 1684. To save expenses, the Qing rulers chose to build a garden at the former site of the well-known private garden of the Ming Dynasty—the Qinghua Garden. Though most of the buildings were severely damaged, trees, hills, pools, springs and stones in the Qinghua Garden were still well preserved. The first imperial garden with man-made hills and river was completed after 3 years' renovation and construction, and was named the Chang Chun Garden. Upon completion, it became an important working location where emperor Kangxi could deal with official affairs. This garden was also the first imperial resort type garden outside the Beijing City in the Qing Dynasty. Later Kangxi gave a Ming private garden north of the Chang Chun Garden to his fourth son, (who later became the emperor Yongzheng) as a "garden of grant", and named it the Garden of Perfect Splendor.

Through years of efforts under Emperor Yongzheng, the area of the Garden of Perfect Splendor as well as the number of buildings inside increased. As Yongzheng spent most of his time in the garden, the Garden of Perfect Splendor became another important imperial resort in the northwest outskirts of Beijing. After being enthroned, Emperor Qianlong still used this garden as his imperial resort. He further expanded and improved the garden on the base of 28 scenic spots completed in the years of Kangxi, and by 1744, the number of scenic spots reached 40. In 1751, Qianlong built the Everlasting Spring Garden on the east and the Yi Chun Garden on the southeast of the Garden of Perfect Splendor. These three gardens that connect to each other were collectively maintained and managed. The Garden of Perfect Splendor evolved into the largest garden in the city suburbs comprising of 3 gardens with an area of 350 hectares.

After the expansion of the Garden of Perfect Splendor was

completed, Qianlong wrote an article, which while giving a description of the beauty and magnificence of the imperial garden, demanded that his descendants stop building more gardens for the sake of saving financial and human resources. But not long after that, he forgot what he said and set about the construction of the Garden of Clear Ripples. Lying in between the Jade Spring Hill and the Garden of Perfect Splendor, the Garden of Clear Ripples was built on the site where the Weng Hill and the west lake are located. The lake had been for years a reservoir that supplied water to the city from the northwest outskirts. So besides the reason of celebrating the birthday of his mother, Emperor Qianlong also stressed that the project could expand the west lake and dredge up the water-supplying tunnel. But the truth lying behind was that this experienced and knowledgeable

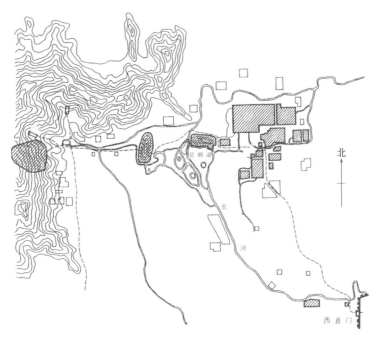

The distributing plan of the gardens in northwest outskirts of Beijing in Qian Long years of the Qing Dynasty

emperor who had a liking for garden construction was not content with either the Fragrant Hills Garden that didn't have a lake or the Garden of Perfect Splendor that was built on flat land without hills. The Weng Hill area turned out to be a perfect place to build a garden as this place had mountains as well as water. Beginning From 1750, supervised by Qianlong himself, the Garden of Clear Ripples was finished in 1764 after 14 years' construction. Till then, there were five imperial gardens in the northwest outskirts of Beijing including the Jing Yi Garden in the Fragrant Hill, the Jing Ming Garden in the Jade Spring Hill, the Garden of Clear Ripples of the Longevity Hill, the Chang Chun Garden and the Garden

Lush trees in the Jingming Garden in the Jade Spring Mountain. Several temples were built here.

The Jing Yi Garden in the Fragrant Hills that harmonizes with the natural landscape

of Perfect Splendor. These five gardens altogether were called "five gardens on three mountains". There were dozens of "gardens of grant" and private gardens scattered around these five gardens. Following the construction of the Garden of Clear Ripples, the clearing up of the water supplying tunnel, the rising of the water level and the increasing of the volume of water flow, a new water sight-seeing route from the Jade Spring Hill to the Kunming Lake, and further through the Chang River arriving at Xizhi Gate inside the city was opened up. Since then, the Haidian District in the northwest outskirts has become a vast imperial garden zone, where different types of imperial and private gardens with natural hills, water, land or artificial hills and water are concentrated. Condensing the garden building tradition of the classic gardens, these gardens serve as examples and classical garden art for later times.

The Appreciation of Some Well-known Gardens

The Imperial Garden of the Forbidden City

Built in the 18th year of the Ming Yong Le period (1420), the imperial garden was finished at the same time as the palatial architecture of the Forbidden City. Some minor reconstruction was made upon completion, but the overall layout was still preserved.

Lying at the northernmost end of the axis of the Forbidden City, the Imperial Garden consists of a group of structures. As this imperial garden is the most important garden with significant location inside the Forbidden City, the designers of the garden didn't adopt the kind of unrestricted and flexible ground layout usually found in private gardens south of the Yangze River. Instead they employed the traditional pattern of bilateral symmetry typical of the palatial architecture.

Structures inside the imperial garden were built in three parallel rows from east to west and the whole garden occupies an area of 1.2 hectares. The Qin An Hall, a Taoist structure, was the center of the garden, where the Yuan Tian God of Daoism was given respect. From south to north in the east row, stands the Jiang Xue Room, the Wan Chun Pavilion, the Fu Bi Pavilion and the Li Zao Hall. Lying at the top of the rockery, the Imperial View Pavilion overlooks the whole garden and the scenes in and outside the

The commanding view-watching spot – The Pavilion of Imperial View in the Forbidden City

Forbidden City. And it was an imperial tradition to climb up to the pavilion and enjoy watching the moon during the Mid-Autumn and the Double Ninth Festival. A cave was dug at the entrance of the hill and water was pumped up high and spouted from the mouth of the stone-carved dragon down the hill. This continuous water flow became one of the scenic spots inside the garden. From south to north in the west row, one can find the Yang Xing Study, the Qian Qiu Pavilion, the Cheng Rui Pavilion, the Wei Yu Study and the Yan Hui Pavilion. This architectural group was symmetrical with the buildings in the east row, and this symmetry formed a very canonical and regular layout of the garden. As the function of the imperial garden differed from the outer court and living quarters of the Forbidden City, the designers and the gardeners, on the premise that the general layout was maintained, employed many flexible garden building techniques to avoid monotony.

First of all, diverse forms and shapes of architecture were adopted. One can see multi-layered pavilions or buildings and single-floor halls as well. The shape of the pavilion also varied from each other. For example, some pavilions are set on top of white marble foundation, while others are bridge pavilions standing above a pool. The lower floor of the Wan Chun Pavilion and the Qian Qiu Pavilion were arranged as a "+" shape, but their upper floors had round roofs with spires. The creation of this new pavilion type combines the magnificence of the imperial architecture with the liveliness of garden construction.

Secondly, the beauty created by the change of minute details can be found at every corner in the layout of bilateral symmetry. The Jiang Xue Room on the East echoes the Yang Xing Study on the West. The former one is a single-floor room with a colored glaze flower platform in front on which flowers and plants are planted and bonsai placed. The latter is a two-floor building half-enclosed by artificial hills. The shape and the scenes they form are different between these two structures. Walking into the

The roof of the Pavilion of Ten Thousands Spring   The roof of the Pavilion of Thousand Autumn

Bonsai of plant fossils in the Imperial garden

imperial garden from the side gates of the Cheng Guang Gate, one will find that the Imperial View Pavilion near the north wall and the Yan Hui Pavilion are in a symmetrical position, however one is a small pavilion on top of the man-made hill, and the other is a two-layer pavilion with roofs covered with glazed tiles. Though similar in shape with the Wan Chun and the Qian Qiu Pavilion, their roofs are different and their pattern of caisson ceilings are also different.

Thirdly, themes and patterns that differ from the palatial construction were used to decorate the buildings. On the surface of the "#" type ceilings of the Fu Bi Pavilion and the Cheng Rui Pavilion, one does not see the usual patterns of dragon and phoenix, instead we see the image of flowers like plum blossom, orchid, peony and fruits such as peach and pomegranate were widely employed. The images are diverse and vivid and some of them signify luck and longevity. Traditional color paintings were not seen on the beams of the Jiang Xue Room, and instead the painters painted a turquoise blue bamboo pattern. In addition, the natural color of wooden doors and windows was left untouched and all these techniques highlighted the beauty of simplicity. This delicate style also can be found in the footpath in the garden. Except for the main path that was built with stone slabs, all other paths were paved with pebbles and bricks. Making use of the different shapes, colors and the texture of stones, the designers made images of animals, flowers, utensils and human figures. Visitors cannot help being captivated by the beauty of these ground "pictures" that spread along the paths.

Fourthly and also the most important technique is the use of plants, flowers, piling rocks and bonsai to decorate the garden environment in order to enhance the natural charm of the garden. Limited by the climate in the north, trees planted are mostly evergreen trees such as pine trees and cypresses. They were planted following the winding of the paths. Deciduous trees such as locust tree, elm and Chinese flowering crabapple are supplementary and are scattered around the garden. These trees create the unique solemn atmosphere of the imperial garden. Flowers are either transplanted or grown in pots. Forsythias, peony and yellow plum would blossom in spring and summer, and chrysanthemums in autumn. Water lilies sleep in the pool. The colorful flowers of different seasons that dot the garden add a touch of glamour to the garden. Some piling rocks are clustered to match the surrounding structures, and others are scattered in corners and these rocks themselves form independent scenes. Except for a few bonsai of precious flowers or plants, most of the bonsai in the garden are rock or stones presented from all over the country. These bonsai vary in shape. Some are exquisitely carved, and others are grand and imposing. The regular and symmetrical layout of buildings and paths is interspersed with plants, flowers, rocks and bonsai, creating a style of solemnity and dignity without losing the natural charm of the garden as well. The Imperial Garden is undoubtedly a masterpiece of garden art.

The Garden of the Tranquility and Longevity Palace

The garden of the Tranquility and Longevity Palace was built as a retreat for Emperor Qianlong after his retirement from active administration, so it is also called the Qian long Garden. Built sometime between 1771–1776, the Tranquility and Longevity Palace consists of two parts-the front and the rear. Buildings in the rear section can be further divided into three rows-middle, east and west row. The garden is located in the west row of the architectural group.

Only half of the size of the Imperial Garden, the Qianlong Garden is limited to a space 160 meters long and 37 meters wide.

The flowing-cup tunnels in the Xi Shang Pavilion

As the area and the shape of the space differ from the Imperial Garden, the gardeners designed a different layout. The designers divided the area, from south to north, into five square courtyards which is the most salient feature of this garden. By doing this, the sense of narrowness of the space is minimized.

Entering the garden from the Yan Qi Gate on the south, visitors will face a manmade hill. Then walking through the winding paths, we see the first courtyard appear in front of our eyes. Facing south, is the main room-the Gu Hua Room which was named after the old birch in front. The east, south and west side of the room are all surrounded with rockeries. The first courtyard features the natural charm of rocks and old trees.

Passing through the Chui Hua Gate on the north of the Gu Hua Room, visitors then enter into the second courtyard. This is a typical quadrangle-type courtyard with the Sui Chu Hall that has the width of five rooms on the north, and flanked by the western and eastern chambers. A veranda connects all the buildings around. Decorated with flowers and plants, this courtyard offers a peaceful and relaxed atmosphere differing from the first courtyard.

Changes can be found in the third courtyard. A huge rockery was placed inside the yard with ridges and peaks stretching out and caves connecting each other. The Song Xiu Pavilion was built at the top. This quiet courtyard boasts of a huge rockery scene, which again offers visitors variety and surprises.

Scenery changes again in the fourth yard. Square-shaped, the

The ceiling with woodcarving in the Gu Hua Hall

imposing and magnificent Fu Wang Pavilion appears right after one enters the gate. Inside the building, partition walls separate it into a maze of compartment rooms. Those walls are decorated with woodcarving, objects inlaid with gold or jade and cloisonné. So exquisite and delicate, these adornments are regarded as one of the decorative wonders in the Forbidden City.

The last courtyard turns to be another yard with regular design. Decorated with cypresses and bamboos, the corner courtyard on the west side forms a separate world of which the main structure is the Bamboo Fragrance Hall. The Juan Qin Hall stands on the north with a width of nine rooms. The four rooms in the west were where the emperor Qianlong enjoyed listening and watching the opera with a small stage set inside. All the interior walls, screens and ceilings were painted with beautiful colored drawings.

As a small-scale imperial garden, the Garden of the Tranquility and Longevity Palace made full use of the Chinese traditional garden building techniques. In terms of ground layout, different shapes of yards and irregular and symmetrical structures were used to form different spaces. In terms of scenery creating, courtyards enclosed by structures and courtyards that gave priority to rockery form different landscapes—one spacious, and the other compact. In terms of architectural form, various forms were used such as halls, storied buildings, storied pavilions, studios, pavilions, etc. In terms of house fitting up and decoration, in addition to glazed tiles, colored drawings and balustrades with carvings, ceilings with woodcarving, gorgeous partition screens and screen walls that were rarely seen in the Forbidden City were used here. Through these techniques, the designers and the gardeners create a garden environment with diversity in a long but narrow space, where each change of vintage point promises you a different view. The Garden of the Tranquility and Longevity is another very refined architectural artwork inside the Forbidden City.

The Garden of Perfect Splendor

Buildings in 120 clusters were counted in the Garden of Perfect Splendor before it was burned into ruins. Small gardens were set inside big gardens, and each was different and with astonishing beauty. The well-known French writer Victor Hugo once commented, "...collecting all the treasures from our churches and the final collection still could not be compared with this luxurious and magnificent architecture". The British royal architect Perth Zhang considered the garden "a lovely architectural complex consisting of the most beautiful and pleasant things in the world". Later he designed the first Chinese style garden in Europe for the Duke of Kent—the Qiu Garden. It was observed that the Garden of Perfect Splendor had had far-reaching influences on the development of the world gardening art.

The Garden of Perfect Splendor was originally the "garden of grant" given by Emperor Kangxi to his fourth son, Prince Yong, who later became the Emperor Yongzheng. During his 13 years of reign, Yongzheng spent most of his time in the garden, and he expanded the garden into an imperial abode with 28 scenic spots. The expansion was continued under Qianlong and the number of scenic spots reached 40. He ordered the construction of two more gardens—the Chang Chun Garden and the Yi Chun Garden and then incorporated these three gardens into one. During the reign of Emperor Jia Qing, he went on expanding the range of the gardens, and ordered more palaces to be built. The Garden of Perfect Splendor finally became the largest imperial garden in the northwest outskirts of Beijing. Occupying an area of 350 hectares, the Garden of Perfect Splendor has a land area of the same size as the Forbidden City and a water area that equals the size of the Summer Palace.

What features does the Garden of Perfect Splendor possess that distinguish it from other imperial gardens? What achievements have been accomplished in terms of the Chinese classical garden construction? The answers can be summarized as follows:

The most salient feature of the Garden of Perfect Splendor is that the garden was built on the site of flatland. This garden featuring landscape of water comprises of many smaller gardens scattered all over the place.

Located on flatland where no hills stand or rivers pass by, the garden boasts of abundance of underground water resource. Water can be found after digging down 3 *Chi* into the earth. (1 meter=3 *Chi*). The designers then decided to build the garden on flatland by making full use of its natural environment. Imitation of natural landscape was created in the garden by digging man-made lakes or pools and piling artificial hills. In this land of 350 hectares, half of the area was dug and transformed into scenes of water, the largest of those being the Sea of Happiness with a width of 600 meters and an area of 30 hectares, a vast expanse

of water surface. There were also middle-sized lakes or ponds 200-300 meters wide and countless small-sized ones. Like flowing ribbons, a web of streams linked all the water bodies into an integrated water system. Earth dug out was piled up into artificial hills. In addition to water scenes, there were large numbers of hills, which accounted for one third of the garden area. But none of these hills was high enough to spoil the beauty of the Garden of Perfect Splendor characterized by a landscape of water.

Though the Garden of Perfect Splendor lies in a place with no natural mountainous environment as that of the Jing Yi Garden in the Fragrant Hills, no peaks rising out from the flatland as that of the Jade Flower Islet in the North Sea Garden and the Longevity Hill in the Garden of Clear Ripples, the designers still created a huge garden with the charm of natural landscape of hills

The painting of the flourishing period of the Garden of Perfect Splendor. In 1974, Qing imperial painter Shen Yuan and Tang Dai painted the silk color painting of the 40 scenes of the Garden of Perfect Splendor. There is only one original painting, which now is collected by the National Library of Paris in France. The painting here is a copy based on historical records.

and lakes by setting small gardens in big gardens and separating the gardens into groups of scenic areas. There were more than 120 scenic spots or areas in different sizes, which were separated by hills but connected through paths and canals. The landscape was full of the flavor of riverside villages of south of the Yangtzi River flavor, with mist and clouds floating on the vast expanse of water and streams and mountain paths wandering gracefully. It was not short walls or winding corridors that separated the scenic spots or areas as those in private gardens, but the winding hills. It was not stone paths or decorative windows that linked, but the wandering and connecting canals and passages. These scenic areas or spots formed "gardens in gardens" of different sizes. These separated as well as connected gardens were integrated and formed a huge garden featuring landscape of water on flatland.

Another characteristic in the landscape construction is the transplanting of scenic spots and historical sites from all over the country. Emperor Qianlong went on six inspection tours

The panoramic view of the three gardens of the Garden of Perfect Splendor today

The destroyed marble boat now anchors at the banks forever.

of China's richest areas in the south, in the course of which he was able to visit numerous scenic spots and famous gardens in Suzhou, Yangzhou and Hangzhou. Paintings of his favorite spots drawn by accompanying royal painter were taken back to Beijing for future imitation. The result was that imitations of six well-known scenic views of the West Lake in Hangzhou, such as "Watching Fish in Jade Spring", "Dancing Lotus in the Courtyard", "Moon Reflected in Three Pools", "Bells Chime in Dusk in Nanping" "Autumn Moon in Peaceful Lake" and "Orioles Sing in Forest of Willows", were built in the Garden of Perfect Splendor in addition to the imitations of Lion Forest Garden, shopping street of Suzhou, the Zhan Garden in Nanjing and the Slender West Lake in Yangzhou.

Something worth mentioning is that there was a group of European style garden structures built under the times of Qianlong. With the spreading of Roman Catholicism in China, Western architectural art and gardening techniques were also introduced into China. These Western style architecture and forms of garden that differed from the traditional Chinese style aroused the interest of the Qing rulers, so Qianlong decided to build a "Western Storied Building" of European palatial style on the north of the Chang Chun Garden. Designed by several missionaries from France, Italy and Bohemia, the Western Storied Building was constructed by Chinese artisans with great precision. This group of structures was completed in the 25th year of Qianlong (1760), including six palatial buildings, such as the Xie Qi Qu, Fang Wai Guan, Hai Yan Hall, Yuan Ying View and three gardens—the Wan Hua Zhang, Xian Fa Hill and the Xian Fa Wall. In the style of Baroque popular in Europe then, the structures were geometrical patterns. Considering the special conditions in China, the designers of the Western Storied Building borrowed some traditional Chinese techniques when designing the layout and architectural forms. For example, the water-spouting tower was built in the shape of a pagoda, the image of birds and beasts replaced the naked human figure sculpture, and some Chinese traditional patterns were also used for the stone decoration. But in general, the Western Storied Building was still a very unique scenic area with strong exotic

The ruins of the Big Fountain in the Garden of Perfect Splendor.

The Jiu Zhou Qing Yan scenic area in the Garden of Perfect Splendor, once the imperial banqueting place, was burnt into ashes in the flames of the Second Opium War.

flavor that differed from the traditional Chinese garden style. This was the first example in Chinese history that Western and Chinese architectural and garden forms and art were combined. This architectural group was no doubt an unprecedented cut practice and courageous breakthrough in a feudalistic country that for a very long time cut itself off the outside world.

The second feature of the construction of the Garden of Perfect Splendor is the diversity and variations in architectural types and forms.

As a large-scale imperial garden complex that served as

temporary imperial headquarters away from the Forbidden City, the Garden of Perfect Splendor had to meet the needs of diverse functions. It was not only a garden for entertainment and rest, but also a palatial complex where the emperor could deal with national political affairs, pay respect to ancestors, worship Buddha and read books. Due to the above reasons, the architectural forms were diverse, including palaces, temples, halls, residence halls, book-storing houses, shopping streets and stages. There were also many pavilions, terraces, storied buildings, storied pavilions built for entertainment and relaxation and service structures such as bridges, docks and piers. Not only using different styles of architectural forms to serve different functions, the gardeners also broke the convention by creating many rarely-seen architectural forms. In addition to the conventional architectural planes such as square, rectangle, there was the shape of the carpenter's square or fan-shaped. Pavilions were also diverse in shape-square, hexagonal, octagonal, circular, cross-shaped and a very special flowing-cup pavilion as well. There were corridors running straight, winding, snaking up hills or declining corridors. Among more than a hundred bridges, one could see many different styles, such as level bridge, winding bridge and arch bridge.

Architectural groups of different sizes formed by these different structures are also diverse. Traditional Chinese architecture were mostly placed in rigid symmetrical order and consisted of typical quadrangle courtyards. Though not transcending this tradition in general, the designers adopted many flexible gardening techniques. Firstly, on the premise of maintaining the general layout of central axis, they used the technique of irregularity in some parts. Secondly, different forms of structures were employed in symmetrical locations. Thirdly, while maintaining the spatial relationship of axis between the main gate and main hall, they arranged other buildings flexibly

The old timely furnishing in the Hall of Dispelling Cloud in the Longevity Hill

according to the natural environments.

Structures inside the garden were all built according to northern official convention. They exemplified a style of imperial dignity with the interiors lavishly decorated and the furnishings tasteful. But in terms of the exterior, except for the imperial court area and a few significant palatial structures, most structures were decorated simply. Either no or only a few colored drawings were used in girders or beams in order to maintain the natural color of woods. Though 120 architectural groups of different size were accounted in this garden, they were not luxurious and majestic in general, but harmonious with the surrounding hills, waters and plants. As a result, a northern garden with a water landscape of was finally created, which was full of the flavor of riverside villages south of Yangtzi River.

The Garden of Clear Ripples (The Summer Palace)

The predecessor of the present Summer Palace, the Garden of Clear Ripples was located between the Jing Ming Garden in the Jade Spring Hill and the Garden of Perfect Splendor. With the Weng Hill and the Weng Hill Lake in front, this perfect environment for building gardens was explored in as early as the Yuan Dynasty.

First built in 1750, based on the Weng Hill and the lake, the garden was designed and built according to the layout of the West Lake in Hangzhou. Emperor Qianlong showed a particular liking to the West Lake, so Hangzhou was always a stop in his six inspection tours to the south of Yangtzi River. In the process of construction, the builders gradually formed a terrain of "hill facing lake and lake embracing hill" by expanding and deepening the lake, and enlarging the Weng Hill with the earth dug out. A long dyke imitating the Su Dyke of the West Lake travels from south to north in the west part of lake. This dyke, together with the inclined branch dyke, divides the lake into three parts. Later, the builders further created a terrain of "hill embedded in lake and lake circling the hill" by digging the Xi River on the north of the hill and connecting it with the lake in front of the hill. After reconstruction, the Weng Hill was renamed the Longevity Hill and the lake was changed into the Kunming Lake. From the layout of the Garden of Clear Ripples, one can see that the spatial relationship between the Longevity Hill and the Kunming Lake, the dividing and the shape of the Kunming lake and the position of the west dyke and its traveling direction are all very similar to the West Lake in Hangzhou.

Most of the scenic spots inside the garden were built around or along the Longevity Hill and the Kunming Lake. On the south foot of the Longevity Hill, the Dispelling Cloud Hall covered with golden-colored glazed tiles shines and the imposing Tower of Buddhist Incense overlooks the whole garden. Climbing up to the Tower of Buddhist Incense and looking far into the distance, one may see the West Dike winding like a green ribbon, the reflection of the 17-Arch Bridge shining in the lake and the three islets—the Han Xu Hall, Zao Jian Hall and Zhi Jing Storied Building standing like the three tripods of an ancient caldron. Along the bank of the lake, there are the well-known Marble Boat, the lifelike Gilt Bronze Ox and the Knowing Spring Pavilion. On the north foot of the Longevity Hill, the architectural group of Four Grand Islets imitating the Tibetan style temple is magnificent and sacred. At the foot of the hill, the lake gradually transforms into a river running slowly and peacefully following the winding of the hill. Banks are covered with thick forest, richly ornamented buildings are hidden in the mist and the structures inside the Suzhou Shopping Street located in the middle part of the Xi River are neatly arranged. Following the running river to the east end, one finds himself in the delicate and graceful Garden of Harmonious Interests when he hears the creeks singing.

Consisting of the imperial court area, the scenic area in front of the hill and the scenic area behind the hill, the Garden of Clear Ripples occupies an area of 290 hectares, of which 75% is water.

The Imperial Court Area

As an imperial garden serving as temporary imperial headquarters, like the Chang Chun Garden and the Garden of Perfect Splendor, the Garden of Clear Ripples had to meet emperors' needs of holding court, so an imperial court area was located right after entering the main gate. Located on the northeast part of the garden and at the southeast foot of the Longevity Hill, this area is facing the lake and near the main gate—East Palace Gate. The reason to choose here on one hand is because that this place is close to the Garden of Perfect Splendor, and it would be convenient for emperors to travel between the two gardens; and on the other hand is because that this layout—lying against the Longevity Hill on the north and facing the Kunming Lake on the east and adjacent to the scenic area—conforms to the convention of "court in front and residence or garden in the rear".

The boat scene of the Qing Yan Boat in the Summer Palace which imitated the shape of western steamboat

The East Palace Gate, located right in front of the imperial area, together with the square, screen walls, decorated archways display a manner of magnificence typical of the imperial architecture. Entering the gate, one immediately faces the architectural group of Hall of Benevolence and Longevity. This hall was the place where emperors held court.

Surrounding the Hall of Benevolence and Longevity, there are several groups of quadrangle courtyards—the Yi Yun House, Yu Lan Hall and the Happiness and Longevity Hall. These are the imperial living quarters that belong to the "back residence" in the convention of imperial court.

Fang

The concept of *fang* (large boat) in Chinese garden architecture, was borrowed from huafang (a gaily-painted pleasure-boat). A fang made of stones is not movable, merely a place to visit, dine or view the landscape. Similar to a boat, the structure of a fang can be divided into three parts including the bow, the midship and the stern. There is a view tower on the bow for visitors to enjoy the scenery. The midship is a sunken structure with long windows on each side, designed for relaxation and dining. At the stern of the fang erect double-layered stairs, the upper part is solid, but the lower part is a fake.

The Scenic Area in Front of the Hill

As the main scenic area occupying 88% of the garden, this area consists of the area south of the Longevity Hill and the complete Kunming Lake area. It can be divided into two parts – the front hill and the front lake.

The Longevity Hill faces south and is adjacent

Overlooking the architectural group of the Hall of Dispelling Cloud and the Pagoda of Buddhist Incense in the Longevity Hill.

to the Kunming Lake. Because of the vast field of vision in front of the hill, the main scenic structures in the garden are concentrated around here. The most significant structure, the Great Gratitude and Longevity Temple built for celebrating the birthday of the empress, was placed in the central part of the front hill. This architectural group comprised of the Heavenly God Hall, the Great Hero Hall, the Hall of Treasures, the Tower of Buddhist Incense, the Zhong Xiang Jie Archway, the Hall of Wisdom of Sea, etc. They were placed starting from the foot of the hill to the ridge in the upper part of the hill, forming a south-north axis. On the two sides of the central axis, there are another two sub-axes. One axis is formed by the architectural group consisting of the Turning Wheel Temple and Kindness and Happiness Storied Building. The other axis is formed by the architectural group consisting of the Treasure and Cloud Storied Pavilion and Arhat Hall. The huge architectural complex built along the three axis towers in the central part of the front Longevity Hill. The imposing Buddhist Incense Tower lying on the high platform and the Sea of Wisdom stand out and form the main body of this complex.

Scores of scenic structures are scattered on both sides of this huge architectural complex. From the lake hill on the eastern ridge of the hill, one can have a good view of the Jade Spring Hill and the "borrowed scene from the West Hill". The Jing Fu Storied Pavilion on the eastern ridge is also where you can overlook the dreamlike Kunming Lake. The Walking in Picture on the west side of the hill, not only creates a visual splendor with its luxurious and magnificent style, but also serves as a good place to enjoy the beautiful structures, the lake and the hill. The Happiness and Longevity Hall on the foot of east side of the hill, together with the waterside Shui Mu Zi Qing, the plaster white decorative walls and their reflections in the lake, produce a natural wonder with the flavor of the waterside village south of

Overlooking the Longevity Hill and the Kunming Lake

the Yangtzi River.

One more outstanding structure is the 728 meter long corridor that travels from east to west on the piedmont of the Longevity Hill. All girders and beams were decorated with colored drawing. The contents of the drawings are very diverse—either stories or scenes from classic novels or animals, plants. Each drawing is unique. Strolling down the Long Corridor, one could enjoy the beautiful view of mountains, lake, and some other scenic spots in the garden. It is not only an outstanding corridor for visitors, but also a colorful gallery.

1600 meters wide and 2000 meters long, the Kunming Lake offers the perfect distance for view watching, which promises the visual effects of the two main scenic areas—the imperial court area and the Longevity hill area.

The designers of Kunming Lake scenic area adopted the layout of "three islets in one lake", of those the most important being the South Lake Islet. There stands a dragon temple named the Guang Run Ancestral Temple in the islet. The 17-arch Bridge, the largest stone bridge in the garden, connects the east side of the islet with the east bank of the lake. Near the east end of the stone bridge a huge double-roofed octagonal pavilion—the Kuo Ru Pavilion—was built. The lateral picture consisting of the islet, bridge and the pavilion forms the most important natural wonder in the garden. The roof and eaves of the Han Xue Hall standing out from the north of the islet echo with the Buddhist Incense Tower across the lake. Standing in the Han Xue Hall, one can enjoy the complete picture of the Longevity Hill, and the towers in the West Hill

borrowing the scenery
As pointed out by a Chinese garden expert Jicheng in *Managing the Garden*, the trick of garden making is *borrowing*. The space is limited whether in an imperial garden or a private one, therefore, garden maker should come up with ways to trigger visitors' horizontal or vertical vision or association, ways to represent the big picture with minor things. Those ways are known as *borrowing the scenery*. The scenery that could be borrowed includes faraway mountains, waters from nearby lakes or rivers, or natural landscape surrounding the garden.

and Jade Spring Hill to the west. Buildings and halls built on the other two islets respectively are not only main sights in the west part of lake, but also good view-watching spots.

The West Dyke of Kunming Lake was built in the same layout of the Su Dyke of the West Lake in Hangzhou with similar position and traveling direction. Like the Su Dyke, six bridges were built. But except one round shape stone arch bridge, on all other bridges different shapes of pavilions were added. These bridge pavilions, like so many pearls, are inlaid in the long dyke.

Scenic Area behind the Hill

During the reconstruction of the Garden of Clear Ripples, the builders expanded the lake in front of the hill, but for the rear part of the hill, they only enclosed it with walls at the hill foot, which restricted the garden from developing further north. But even in this long but narrow space, with painstaking design and management, they still created a very unique landscape.

The landmark in the rear hill area, the Hou Xi River traveling

The lavishly decorated Long Corridor

Xu Mi Ling Jing Lama Temple

The restored Shopping Street

from west to east, was dug on the north piedmont of the Longevity Hill. Earth dug out was piled up into small hills, and formed a layout of "two hills nipping one river in the middle". Limited by the natural environment, the river way couldn't be too wide. In this narrow watercourse of 1000 meters long, the designers deliberately dug the river in different width ranging from 10 to 70 meters.

Another special scenic spot is the shopping street lying at the middle of the Xi River that imitates the style of business streets in Suzhou and Nanjing. In this 270-meter- long riverside shopping street, shops stand side by side on both banks with flags flying in the wind. When emperors came, eunuchs would be disguised as shop assistants and customers. Seeing this bustle in the street, one would wonder if he had come to the downtown busy streets of a southern waterside village.

Like the area in front of the hill, dozens of architectural groups were built in the relatively slow back hill slope, of those the most important being the Xu Mi Ling Jing Temple in the center of the back hill. As the largest Buddhist architecture in the imperial garden, the temple not only met the needs of emperor's Buddha

A panoramic view of the refined and compact Garden of Harmonious Interests

worshipping, but also served the function of showing goodwill to the Tibetan and Mongolian minorities. In the rear part of the temple, a huge religious architectural group imitating the form of the famous Sang Ye Temple in Tibet was built.

To compare the landscape between the front and back hill scenic areas, one could clearly see that views in the front hill area are vast and open, and views in the back hill are peaceful and introvert.

At the northeast foot of the Longevity Hill, there is a small and relatively independent "garden in a garden" that imitates the Ji Chang Garden in Wuxi.

Similar to the Ji Chang Garden, the Garden of Harmonious

Interests is also centered around a pond. Clusters of rockery on one side of the pond together with the structures on the other side form a small close space. The pond in the middle of the garden has the similar size of the water surface of the Ji Chang Garden. On one corner, the Knowing Fish Bridge that imitates the Knowing Fish Hall in the Ji Chang Garden is suspended above the water and forms little bays. The technique used and the position of bridge is same as the Seven Stars Bridge in the Ji Chang Garden. On the north bank of the garden, designers introduced the Xi River water into the rockery and using the drop in water level made the Yu Qin Xia Natural Flow with successive layers, achieving the same visual and acoustics effect as that of the Ba Yin Jian in the Ji Chang Garden. The present Han Xue Hall was added later. Now the Seeking Poem Path circling around the rockery on the northeast of the Han Xue Hall still maintains the original atmosphere of serene mountainous path.

Though many different architectural forms are used in the

Overlooking the architectural groups on the south and north sides of the Longevity Hill

Garden of Harmonious Interests, such as pavilion, waterside pavilion and corridor, there are no repetitions. In terms of pavilions, there are square, round, double-roofed pavilion and long pavilion surpassing above the water. As for corridors, there are hollow corridors, corridors following the wall, folding corridors, arc-shaped corridors, water corridors, etc. Though still maintaining the northern official architectural convention, the garden avoids the solemnity typical in the imperial architecture. Decorated with rockery, pond and plants, it has the delicate style of the gardens in the South. Corridors that connect all the structures form a visiting route circling around the pond. Strolling inside the corridors and looking around, one could watch all kinds of pictures framed by the beams and pillars of the pavilion, waterside pavilion and corridor. In April of the spring, sprouts of green willow trees touch the water. The scenery is even more enchanting in hot July of summer with lotus and water lily blossoms covering the pond.

The Summer Palace, the last imperial garden built in the history of China, is a melting pot of natural landscape and man-made wonders, and the magnificence of the imperial garden and the delicacy of the garden in the south. It reaches a very high level in terms of general ground plan, designing, creativity and the diversity of the scenic spots and displays the great achievements in garden construction of the Qing Dynasty.

The Mountainous Summer Resort in Chengde

The Mountainous Summer Resort in Chengde, commonly known as the Chengde Summer Palace, was originally called the Rehe Imperial Abode. Located in the north part of the Chengde city, it is the largest imperial garden still existing in China and a well-known historical scenic area that occupies an area of 5,640,000 square meters. The construction took 87 years starting from the 42nd year of Kangxi's reign (1704) and was completed in the 55th year of Qianlong (1790). More than 120 structures including storied buildings, terraces, halls, storied pavilions, studies, pavilions, waterside pavilions, temples, pagodas, corridors and bridges are constructed, of those 36 have Emperor Kangxi's imperial inscription. In the 16th year of Qianlong (1751), expansion was carried out and 36 scenic spots nominated by Qianlong were finished. In addition, 8 temples, arranged in a shape of arch, were successively built on the east bank of the Wu Lie River outside the resort. A huge ancient architectural complex consisting of imperial court, temple and garden had gradually taken shape.

in the convention of "court in front and garden in the rear", the resort is divided into two parts—imperial court area in the front and the garden area in the rear. The garden area is further divided into the lake area, plain area and hill area according to the different physiognomy and sights.

The Imperial Court Area

Located in the south of the resort, the imperial court area consists of three parallel groups of palatial structures. The Zheng Palace, the main body of the area, consists of 9 courtyards divided into two parts: the front court and the back living quarters. The Zheng palace was where emperors managed the state affairs, read and resided in, the most well-known building being the Yan Bo Zhi Shuang Hall, which is the main hall of living quarters in the Zheng Palace and also serves as the imperial sleeping palace of the Qing emperors. It is located in a place high and spacious, and embraced on four sides by rolling hills. In hot summer, cool wind blowing from peaceful lake brings pleasant coolness, so this structure was named Yan Bo Zhi Shuang Hall by Kangxi meaning "lake brings coolness" and was listed the top scenery among the 36 Kangxi nominated scenic spots.

As far as the number and the scale of the palatial architectural

The Zhan Bo Jing Cheng Hall in the imperial court area

group in the imperial court area are concerned, the Summer Resort in Chengde no doubt is the largest imperial garden, however, all structures are very harmonious with the surroundings. In terms of the architectural form, the structures are wide consisting of many bays, but they are not lofty. Houses are connected by corridors to keep the structures low and extended. In terms of the decoration, the builders used gray tiles for the roof instead of glazed tiles, and the natural color of wood or simple color instead of colored drawings on girders, beams, doors and windows. Even the most significant Zhan Bo Jing Cheng Hall is no exception. It is refined but not luxurious. All girders, beams, windows and doors were made by nanmu of natural color, and windows and doors were decorated with woodcarving. Great efforts were made in the arrangement of the courtyard to achieve the atmosphere of primitive simplicity with pine trees scattered around the courtyard setting off by piling rocks. The builders made use of the natural stone to build the foundation or slope for the Pine and Crane Hall and the last hall of the East Palace to form a smooth transition between the imperial court area and the garden area.

During the time of Kangxi and Qianlong's reign, emperors' inspection tours and hunting activities were always accompanied by a large crowd of court officials and military generals. Emperors afterwards who spent summer in resort were also accompanied by imperial concubines. The resort actually became another political center outside the capital city.

The Lakes Scenic Area

One feature of the Summer Resort is that its layout was designed based on the natural hill and water in the garden. Located in the southeast of the resort, the lakes area occupies an area of 43 hectares. Similar to the Garden of Perfect Splendor, this garden, also built on the site of flatland, features largely on water scenery. The lakes area consists of eight man-made islets and eight lakes big or small interconnected by dyke, dam, watercourse and bridge. Only one tenth of the whole resort area, this lakes area concentrates half of the structures of the whole garden. They were built on different islets respectively. The Ru Yi Islet, Moonlight and River Music and the Lion Forest in Wen Garden are some of the large ones. Before the completion of the Zheng Palace, the Ru Yi Islet was the place where emperors managed state affairs and resided in. The Moonlight and River Music served as study and resting place for empresses. The Lion Forest in Wen Garden, lying southeast of the resort, was a beautiful "garden set in garden" enclosed with rockery, which imitated the Lion Forest in Suzhou.

A view of the water pavilion

The most important scenic structures in the lake area are two architectural groups—the Gold Hill Pavilion and the Cloud and Rain Storied Building. Built on a small islet on the east bank of the Cheng Lake in the east of the lakes area, the pavilion was named the Gold Hill Pavilion because of its similarity with the Jiang Tian Temple in the Gold Hill in Zhenjiang, Jiangsu Province in terms of the topography and architectural form. Like a mountain peak towering on the bank of the Cheng Lake, the Gold Hill Pavilion not only is a beautiful scenic spot on its own, but also a good view-watching spot from where one could overlook the lake, plains on the west and north side and the mountainous landscape. Named after a scenic spot of same name in Nan Lake in Jiaxing, Zhejiang Province because of the similar topography and surrounded by water, the Cloud and Rain Storied Building stands in a small islet north of the Ruyi Islet, the largest islet in lakes area, and offers vast field of vision. The Cloud and Rain Storied Building is a group of courtyards. Looking at each other

A close look of the Cloud and Rain Storied Building

across the lake, the Cloud and Rain Storied Building and the Gold Hill Pavilion form "echoing sights" on east and north.

Alternating between water and islet, and connected by dyke and bridge, the lake area displays a strong appeal of Southern China waterside village. The lake area is not as spacious and open as the Garden of Perfect Splendor or the front scenic area of the Summer Palace, but it offers richer layers of landscape set off by the mountainous landscape area and the plain scenic area. Though lacking magnificent scenic wonders like the Longevity Hill or the Tower of Buddhist Incense, the lakes area shows a more friendly and delicate atmosphere with islets connected by dykes, lotus and water lily blossoms covering the lake, willows turning green and flowers giving off aroma.

The Plain Scenic Area

A piece of long but narrow flatland north of the lake area, the plain scenic area is about the same size as that of the lake area. In

The natural transition from the plain area to the mountainous area

the east part of the plain area, there lies the Ten Thousand Trees Garden where thousands of elms were planted and flocks of elks raised in the forest. In the western part, there is the Trial Riding Land where grasses are thick as blankets, displaying a view of roughness north of the Great Wall.

A unique area in the resort, the plain area served as not only field banqueting sites outside the palace for emperors, but also important places for political activities. In 1771, Qianlong received Wobaxi, leader of the Tuerhute Tribe, who submitted to Qing rulers. Qianlong wrote the epigraphs for the two stone tablets—*Tuerhute Tribe's Submitting* and *Comforting and Compensating the Tuerhute Following*. The tablets were still standing in the Pu Tuo Ancestral Temple outside Chengde city.

At the northeast corner of the plain area, there is the Everlasting Blessing Temple standing alone in a quiet corner of the Ten Thousand Trees Garden. The orange colored tower body of the 9-story Pagoda inside the temple looks very striking under the blue sky. South of the lake area, four pavilions were built along the banks. They were named, from west to east, the Shui Liu Yun Zai, Hao Pu Jian Xiang, Ying Zhuan Qiao Mu and Pu Tian Cong Yue. Varying in shape, these pavilions are larger than normal pavilion in order to match the environment. Standing along the banks as good view-watching spots, they also serve as good transitions between the north and south scenic areas, so that scenic areas of different landscapes can be integrated into a harmonious whole.

The Mountainous Landscape Area

This area occupies the complete northwest part of the resort, about four fifth of the resort's area. It boasts of smooth rolling hills without odd peaks or dangerous cliffs, the hills covered with fertile soil and lush trees. In order to meet the needs of view watching, visiting and residing, the builders paved mountain

Primitive and rough scenery of the mountainous area of the Summer Resort.

paths vertically and horizontally and scattered more than 20 architectural groups of temples and gardens.

More than 20 temples or garden structures are scattered sparsely everywhere in the mountainous area. Except for the four of them standing on the mountaintop, all others are hiding in the valleys. Halls, storied buildings, pavilions and corridors were arranged flexibly following the changes of topography. What the designers sought was the harmony between architecture and nature, so structures are not large in size, and the exteriors are not luxurious but simple and natural.

Four pavilions were built on four mountaintops and named respectively—the Cloud on Four Sides, the Hammer Peak in Evening Glow, the Snow on Mt. Nan and the Resting on Two North Peaks. Standing on the northwest peak, the Cloud on Four Sides Pavilion with a high altitude offers a good view of the rich and varied rosy clouds rising slowly in rolling hills several hundreds li away (1km=2 *li*). When the sun set off, from the Hammer Peak in Evening Glow Pavilion located at the southwest peak, one could enjoy the red rays of evening glow covering the sky and the huge golden color stone in Chime Hammer Peak towering against the sky like a beautiful paper-cut. The Snow on Mt. Nan and the Resting on Two North Peaks Pavilions are located north of the lakes and plain area, and form the main "echoing scenic spots" when one look north in the garden. After the winter snow, overlooking the lake from the Snow on Mt. Nan Pavilion, one would be impressed by the fairyland-like landscape of pavilions and structures covered with white snow, and reflected in ice lake.

The Summer Resort embodies four scenic areas in one resort— the imperial court area consisting of courtyards and architectural groups; the lakes area full of the Southern China riverside village flavor; the plain area showing the sights of grassland north of the Great Wall and the north hill area with imposing mountainous landscape. Landscapes are different in each area and each of them has distinguishing features, but each shines more brilliantly in the other's company. The practice of melting the southern and northern landscapes and charm in one garden was seldom employed in other gardens.

The scenic area of Summer Resort not only includes the resort itself, but also its surroundings, the most well known of those being the Outer Eight Temples.

The Outer Eight Temples

Built in the rolling hills east and north of the resort, the Outer Eight Temples consist of in fact not eight but twelve temples. They were generally named the Outer Eight Temples because that firstly eight of them had lamas dispatched by imperial court to stay in and paid by the Border Affairs Department, and secondly the temples are located north of the Great Wall. Mainly in the style of Tibetan Buddhist temples, the Eight Outer Temples were built in the "flourishing age of Emperor Kangxi and

Overlooking the Putuo Buddhist Temple from the Summer Resort in Chengde

Qianlong". With consummate building techniques and different styles, they are a fine example of the fusion of Han, Mongolian and Tibetan cultures. Here one could feel the magnificence of the Potala Palace in Tibet, the grandeur of the Tashilhungpo Monastery in Xikaze the charm of the Shuxiang Temple in Mt. Wu Tai and the shine of Guerzha Temple in Yili, Xingjiang province. The world's largest wooden Buddhist figure— Bodhisattva Guanyin with one thousand hands and eyes, was placed here also. In terms of the exteriors, structures in the resort, no matter the magnificent imperial palaces or the pavilions, waterside pavilions, halls for entertainment, were all built with grey bricks and tiles displaying a style of primitive simplicity. In contrast, the surrounding outer Eight Temples were covered with colored glazed tiles, and some even with fine gold colored fish scale tiles overspreading the roof. When one looks from afar, the vision of magnificence, resplendence and splendor of the Outer Eight Temples will form a strong contrast with the primitive simplicity and elegance of the Summer Resort. The construction of these temples in the Qing Dynasty showed their respect toward the Tibetan Buddhism worshipped by Tibet and Mongolian minorities, but more importantly it was to strengthen the relationship between Tibet, Mongolian people and the central government in order to avoid the dispute and rebellions in borders. We could see that it carried more political significance than religious meanings.

The Comparison between Imperial Gardens and Private Gardens

Imperial gardens and private gardens are two major types of classic Chinese gardens. There are similarities as well as differences between them.

Both types of gardens feature man-made landscapes and serve the function of entertainment and rest, but due to the differences between the life of their owners and the corresponding requirements on gardens, they also differ in functions. Private gardens are mostly attached to the residence, so they have the places for residing, receiving guests, reading and entertaining. In imperial gardens, in addition to these functions, temples for emperors to worship ancestors and Buddha are also

The delicate wooden arch bridge crossing over the little stream in the Mind Cultivating Study (Jing Xin Study) in the North Sea Park.

Light and primitively simple water pavilion in the Ji Chang Garden in Wuxi

indispensable parts of the garden. For imperial gardens that also serve as temporary headquarters away from Forbidden City, because emperors spend most of time there, the imperial court area for emperors to hold court is added. Besides, in terms of entertaining area, the big opera tower, the shopping street, the pavilion or terrace for watching fireworks, fields for cultivating and places for planting mulberry and silkworm breeding are not available in private gardens.

In terms of garden planning and scenery creating, imperial gardens and private gardens both adopt the techniques of imitating and symbolism in order to recreate natural landscapes

The magnificent and elegant 17 Arches Bridge in the Summer Palace

in a limited space. But because of the differences in land area and the poetic realms their owners seek, imperial gardens and private gardens present different outlooks and views. With an area of several hectares, tens of *mu*, or just several *mu*, private gardens seek to "present the feeling of greatness through small details". The designers designed more winding paths and secret scenic spots. They sought to separate the limited space into diverse small worlds by making full use of the rockery, hollow corridor and small walls. No matter large structures such as a hall or a pavilion, or small decorations such as a rock or a bamboo, they all stand as independent scenic spots. By doing these, macro poetic realm can be felt through micro scenes. In contrast, except for the Imperial Garden inside the Forbidden City, the area of other imperial gardens is at least more than scores of hectares. In such a huge space, the designers must make some big projects.

Huge scenic areas with different characteristics were created, for example, some gardens were built taking advantage of natural hill and lake, and others were created by digging man-made lake and piling earth into hills or dykes. In contrast with the natural, delicate and simple style typical in private gardens, scenes in imperial gardens are generally vast and spacious and structures are magnificent, which fully display the dignity and the splendor of imperial gardens.

One may find a phenomenon from the imperial gardens introduced above that many scenic spots were built according to the models of famous scenes or private gardens in Southern China. It was normal that the construction of imperial gardens absorbed or adopted the building techniques from all over the country because imperial construction inevitably concentrated the best techniques and men of talents. In order to build the Forbidden City, the Ming Emperor Yong Le recruited ten thousand artisans including many skillful craftsmen from the south of China. South China landscape painter Ye Zhao

Five Old Men Listening to the Zither in the Gu Yi Garden in Nanxiang. The five lake rocks represent the five old men and the stone table is the zither support.

participated in the planning of Chang Chun Garden. Rockery making master Zhang Ran was in charge of the rock-piling project of the Chang Chun Garden, which was Kangxi's first imperial garden in northwest outskirts of Beijing. Through efforts of these artisans and masters, the techniques of structure building and gardening from Southern China were introduced to the north and combined with the northern techniques. But transplanting certain garden scenic spots completely into imperial garden was not something that could be realized by ordinary artisans, because it required the understanding of garden owners or planners' pursue. On these aspects, one could not neglect the influences of the two garden art lovers – Emperor Kangxi and Qianlong. Especially under the supervision of Qianlong, large number of scenic spots imitating scenes and gardens in Suzhou and Hangzhou appeared in the building and expanding of the Garden of Perfect Splendor and the Mountainous Summer Resort. The Garden of Harmonious Interests imitating the Ji Chang Garden in Wuxi was built in the Garden of Clear Ripples as well. The construction of imperial gardens, like imperial palatial architecture, concentrated refined building techniques and talented artisans and workers from all over the country, therefore, gardening masterpieces with highest level of technical and artistic achievements in its times could be created.

Garden Building Masters and Theories on Creating a Garden

This painting *The Spring Field Trip* created in the 6th century is a work of early Chinese landscape painting, which evokes profound artistic realm of the natural mountain and water.

The cover of the *Craftsmanship of Gardening*

The classic Chinese garden first appeared in the Qin and Han Dynasties, was founded in the Wei-Jin and South-North Dynasties, developed in the Tang Dynasty, matured in the Song Dynasty and reached its peak in the Ming and Qing Dynasties. During the longstanding development of Chinese classical garden, countless talented artisans contributed their painstaking efforts to these beautiful landscape gardens, and Zhang Nanheng was one of them. Alternately named Zhang Lian, he was born in Huating in Jiangsu Province in the 15th year of Wan Li's reign in the Ming Dynasty. He studied painting in his early years and later he embedded the realm of Chinese landscape painting into his garden building practices. A rock or a tree would show unique interests through his designing and arrangement. Being expert in making rockery, he didn't strive to simply imitate the shape of big mountains, but to seek the essences of the natural hills or mountains. An artificial hill with sinuous caves and distant peaks he created in a garden of a very limited space could evoke one's dream life of secluding in mountains and forests. His son Zhang Ran carried on his father's career, and was called in by Emperor Kangxi to Beijing to participate in the rockery project in the imperial West Garden, Jade Spring Hill Garden and the Chang Chun Garden. Later, family Zhang's descendants settled in Beijing and devoted themselves in creating rockery. With techniques handed down through generations, family Zhang gradually became famed rockery family in north China-Rockery Zhang.

Scholars' participation in the making of gardens enriched the external beauty and the cultural connotations of gardens. Based on practices, they contributed a bulk of theoretic books on garden construction, which provided penetrating summary and elaboration on the Chinese garden art. Some important examples are *One School's Opinion* by Li Yu, *Records on Surpluses* by Wen Zhenheng and *Craftsmanship of Gardening* by Ji Cheng. Li Yu was born in the Qiantang River area of Zhejiang in the 39th year in Wan Li's reign in the Ming Dynasty (1611). He once visited scenic spots and gardens all over the country and also took part in the planning and designing of garden. One volume of *One School's Opinion* discusses the theory on architecture and garden construction. A descendant of famed Ming painter Wen Zhengming, Wen Zhenheng was born in Changzhou, (presently Wu county) Jiangsu province in the 13th year of Wan Li in the Ming Dynasty (1585). Four volumes of *Records on Surpluses* have contents related with garden making.

Born in the 10th of year of Wan Li in the Ming Dynasty (1582), Ji Cheng was from Wujiang, Jiangsu Province. He was fond of art when he was a child and later became expert in calligraphy and painting, which helped him accomplish great artistic achievements in garden building. He traveled extensively in China and was a practitioner of garden construction. In 1634, the 7th year of Chong Zhen in the Ming Dynasty, at the age of 52, he finished the writing of *Craftsmanship of Gardening*, a monograph about garden construction.

Chen Congzhou

Chen Congzhou (1998-2000), the famed contemporary Chinese expert on ancient architecture and gardening art, was from Hangzhou city, Zhejiang province. His early research was devoted to literature and history, and he was an accomplished artist on traditional Chinese painting, poetry and essays. Later he engaged himself in research and teaching of ancient architecture and gardening art. Once a professor and doctoral supervisor of Tongji University, he manifested remarkable insight into garden making. He once remarked: "Garden making has rules but no formula. The art constantly evolves, new and creative ideas compete for attention. The garden rises to prominence because of its scenery, the scenery achieves distinction because of the garden it belongs." In 1978, Mr. Chen went to New York City to design and build a garden named *Mingxuan* for the Metropolitan Museum of Art. In 1987, he took charge of the designing and construction of the renovation project of the eastern garden of *Yuyuan* Garden in Shanghai. His writings on gardening, such as *Suzhou Gardens*, *Yangzhou Gardens*, *Collections of Gardening*, *Essays on Gardening*, were undoubtedly Chinese contemporary classical works on gardening art research.

The painting of *Nanjing Zhan Garden* by a Qing painter

This book comprehensively elaborates the theory and practice on Chinese garden, including planning, designing, construction of houses, forms of door, window, wall and floor, choosing of the stone materials, making rockery, etc. It is the most important ancient theoretical book on garden building in China. The book is divided into three volumes and can be summarized into contents of the following three fields:

Contents on garden building techniques and garden-related knowledge occupy the largest proportion of the book. For example, in the chapter of "Zhuang Zhe", he listed 62 types of wooden door leaf in words and illustrations; in the chapter of "balustrade", he listed more than a hundred forms of balustrade; and in the chapter of "wall", he introduced the forms, features, materials used, building techniques and the applicable occasions of all different types of wall. Illustrations of some wall forms were attached. These vivid and concrete materials with excellent pictures and accompanying essay were the result of long-term

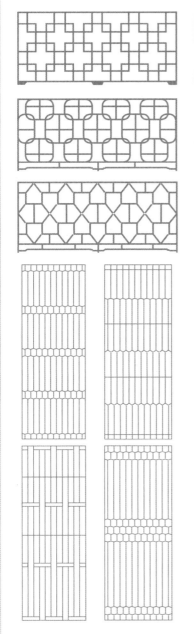

Patterns of separating screen and balustrade recorded in the *Craftsmanship of Gardening*

collection of practical resources and systematic sorting and generalization, which is hardly seen in other theoretical books on gardening.

Summary of garden building experiences, another important part of the book, appears in the beginnings of almost all volumes and chapters. In the piece of writing called "analyzing the environment" in the first volume of *Craftsmanship of Gardening*, Ji Cheng analyzed the characteristics of different garden-building environment such as mountain forest, city, village, fields, place beside the residence, and brought forward corresponding garden-building principles. In the chapter of "wall", the author summarized that the building materials for outer and inner walls of the garden should be refined and appropriate and selected flexibly according to the change of locations. More were written on "making rockery" and "stone selection". He summed up 17 optimal shapes of rockery. He also listed 16 types of stone materials including the most precious Tai Hu Rock, moorstone and common yellow stone, and further explained their morphological features and optimal ways of using.

Theoretical elaboration on garden making is the essence of this book.

Ji Cheng made pointed theoretical summarization on garden composition, the principles and techniques of scenery creating. He brought forward the important principle that "there are general rules, but no fixed formulae". He believed that construction of a garden should conform to its own features, but should not adhere to any fixed pattern, and orderliness should be contained in complexity. He also pointed out that the building of a garden should follow principles of nature. No matter in city or village, each step of garden construction should try to be "much more natural, though man-made", which is to say that the uppermost realm of Chinese gardening is to achieve the illusion of real nature in manmade landscape gardens.

This garden-building master made systematic theoretical summarization and elaboration on practical experiences of the past in Chinese garden art. He pinpointed the relationship of essential elements such as style, form, color, texture and types of scenery, so that there were rules to follow in scenery creating, spatial relationship arrangement, scenic spot composition and almost all other fields in garden making. These theories on garden making are regarded as the most reasonable and effective principles and techniques in creating a Chinese classical garden. Garden builders consider it the highest realm to skillfully master all these garden artistic rules.

The summarization and elaboration on theory of garden making of course mark the high level of the artistic achievements in Chinese garden art, but when these creative artistic principles become conventionalized techniques that people of later generations have to follow, rules of art would become fixed patterns of art. Over-ossified and over-artificial works of low quality would then inevitably appear because of the substantive increase in philistinism and disharmony, which are elements against the natural charm of garden.

How to Appreciate the Beauty of Gardens' Artistic Conception (Realm)

The Creation of Gardens' Artistic Conception (Realm)

Artistic realm is the implications and realm conveyed through images or figures in the ancient Chinese artistic creation. Especially in poetry and painting, whether there is an artistic realm or whether the realm is high or low become important standards for artwork appreciation. For ancient painting, artists in their artwork should not only depict the tangible "realm of substance" in objective world, but also demonstrate certain thoughts or feelings, which are what ancient people called "emotional realm" or the "artistic realm". In a classical garden, especially a scholar's garden, shallow pond with green water, lotus, water lily, bamboo, bright moon and cool breeze are all important components of scenery in a garden. A garden that is full of poetic charm and imaginary space, simple but elegant, pure and fresh is considered to be the top grade. When a garden owner builds a garden, he will place his spiritual pursuit into the scenes of garden, hoping that visitors will be sympathetic and emotionally touched by these scenes. So in order to fully appreciate the beauty of a garden, one should also fix his attention on the general artistic realm behind scenes to understand the implied philosophy and view of life.

Symbolism and Allegories

Confucius said that "the wise take pleasure in the water, and the kind find happiness in a mountain". The idea contained in this apothegm that wisdom is as comprehensive as water that could contain infinity and kindheartedness is as firm as a mountain from which everything could grow, is widely accepted in later times.

In this sense, garden owners' actions of digging lake and making rockery represent not only their fondness of natural environment, but also their longing and pursuit for virtues and wisdom. Emperor Qin Shi Huang made the Chang Pond by leading the Wei River

The scene viewed from the garden window

to Xianyang, and built the Penglai Sacred Mountain in the pond to pray for the blessing of supernatural being. This practice of building symbolic immortal islet or sacred mountain had always been employed frequently in later ages, for example, the three islets built in the Taiye Pond of the Jian Zhang Palace in Chang'an in the Han Dynasty; the Peng Lai Islet built in the Taiye Pond in the Grand Ming Palace in Chang'an in the Tang Dynasty; the three islets in the Taiye Pond in imperial city in the Grand Capital in the Yuan Dynasty, the Peng Islet and Yao Hill in the Sea of Happiness, the largest lake in the Garden of Perfect Splendor and the three islets in the Kunming lake in the Summer Palace in the Qing Dynasty. We could see that the devout belief in landscape's symbolic meaning never faints in later times.

Learning from Nature
Learning from nature, in the perspective of garden making, contains two meanings. One is that the overall layout and combination should be in line with the nature. The relation between water and hill, the arrangement of the peak, gully, slope and cave in a rockery, should comply with the law of nature. The second is that every element of the garden should be arranged in certain way according to the nature. For example, the ridge and peak of a rockery are piled up by tiny little stones in a way imitating the natural texture of rocks, meanwhile, traces of artificial stacking should be eliminated to the least; the pond should wind or rise or fall in natural way; the arrangement of plants should be in uneven density and natural way.

Ancient people also projected their recognition of Confucianism onto plants in nature. Pine trees are mighty and sturdy, bamboos are straight and gnarled and plums blossom in cold winter. Their stances and natural habits associate people with temperaments or characteristics such as lonliness, chastity and tenacity. So Chinese scholars consider pine, bamboo and plum blossoms as "the three friends in frostiness" to signify the exalted human character, thus the three plants become the usual carriers in Chinese poetry, painting and even gardening. Artists chant verses or portray these images to assimilate themselves or to show their admiration for these noble characters. For example, the most important mountain path in the mountainous area of the Summer Resort is the pine-covered Pine Cloud Gorge. Scholars like the straight and gnarled stance of bamboo, so almost all private gardens south of Yangtzi River are decorated with bamboos. Bai Juyi, a poet who favored bamboo, not only wrote many poems about the bamboo, but also planted many bamboos in his own private garden. Su Shi, an eminent writer in the Song Dynasty, was famed for his affection to bamboo. "It is possible to dine without meat, but cannot live without bamboo", he once wrote, "eating no meat makes people thin, but without bamboo people will become vulgar".

Lotus roots are fragile, but they can grow high out of silts segment after segment. Water lilies grow from mud, but they blossom beautifully out of water. These eco-features of lotus and water lily no doubt embody profound life philosophy and signify the noble characters and virtues people should possess in a stagnant social environment. So lotus and water lily, like pine, bamboo and plum blossom, always appear in paintings and garden. They not only decorate the picture and environment with their beautiful appearance, but also purify people's hearts with their artistic implications. In the Garden of Perfect Splendor, lotus flowers cover the pond in a scenic spot called "Lian Xi

Yue Chu"and Qianlong inscribed, "there are men of honor everywhere". The designers of the Humble Administrator's Garden made full use of the double functions of water lily and lotus in image and cultural connotations. Lotus and water lily they planted covered the pond in front of the main hall and the hall was named the Fragrance Spreading Far Hall because the fragrance of lotus is light and could be spread to far away. They built a pavilion beside the lotus pond in the west of the garden, and named the Lingering and Listening Hall, which was quoted from Li Shangyin's sentence of "keep the remnant lotus for listening to the rain". When summer passes and autumn comes, one can sit in the pavilion silently and listen to the sound of rain dropping on the leaves of the lotus.

Seek Poetic Mood and Artistic Realm

The artistic realm and the outlook presented by gardens are mainly the results of the artistic attainments of garden owners,

The scene in the Orchid Pavilion where scholars flew wine cup in winding water and chanted verses portrayed by painter

which was also why so many famous gardens were built or designed by scholars or painters, and famed gardening masters were almost all good at painting. Building a garden has similar aesthetic standard and spiritual request as chanting verses or drawing paintings. The building of a garden often comes from literary inspirations. The interests and charm of a garden depend even

The natural marble painted screen and the stele that hints the theme of the scenery in Spring Flower and Autumn Moon House in Nan Garden in Anning

more on words to transfer. Gardening, poetry, calligraphy and painting influence, infiltrate and supplement each other.

The usage of poems, verses and ballads in gardens can be found in the inscriptions – to describe the scenery using elegant words and to reveal the artistic realms. Inscriptions are the best specifications for gardens. Good inscriptions, such as the nomination of a scenic spot and the couplets hung on the columns of hall, not only adorn hall or waterside pavilion, decorate window and door, enrich views, but also express emotions and feelings of garden builders and owners.

First built in the Southern Song Dynasty, the Master-of-Nets Garden was originally named the Fisherman's Seclusion, representing garden owner's pursuit of a private life. In the Qing Dynasty, the garden was renamed the Master-of-Nets Garden. Master of nets still carries the original meaning of fisherman. In the west part of the Humble Administrator's Garden in Suzhou, there stands a waterside pavilion. In the still of night, cool breeze blows gently and bright moon hung in the sky is reflected in water, displaying a serene atmosphere. Quoting from Su Shi's verse "with whom to sit, bright moon, cool breeze and me", the garden owner named the pavilion "with whom to sit", which accurately states the artistic realm of this scenic spot and also signifies the exclusive character of the garden owner.

According to *Zhuang Zi Autumn Water*, Zhuang Zi, an ancient philosopher and Hui Shi once stopped by the side of a pond.

Zhuang Zi said: "Fish swim to and fro in the water, what happy fish!" Hui Shi asked: "You are not a fish, how do you know they are happy?" Zhuang Zi replied: " You are not me, how do you know I don't know?"

This dialogue, full of wisdom and humor, was extensively quoted in many garden works in later times. Such as the Knowing Fish Hall in the Ji Chang Garden, the Knowing Fish Bridge in the Garden of Harmonious Interests, the Knowing Fish Fosse in Jing Yi Garden in the Fragrant Hill, etc. They all seek a life of happiness, content and freeness.

Couplet hung on the columns of a hall in garden structures

Adapting working methods to local conditions, designers and builders created many unique gardens. Though differing from each other, these gardens share one similarity—wherever you stand in the garden, you will have fresh visual surprises. Chinese gardeners pay much attention to the graduation of views, the composition of structures; the supporting of rockeries and ponds and the decoration of the flowers and trees in order to create the poetic mood and artistic realm. To fully comprehend the pictorial and poetic charm of gardens, one not only has to be familiar with the usual techniques and layouts of Chinese gardens, but also sees into the delicate and aesthetic cultural taste behind the scenes with his heart.

Since the Yuan Dynasty, Chinese gardening has been closely related with painting. Techniques of gardening share similarities with painting techniques and this point can be reflected mainly in the fields of water-view-creating and rockery-making. For example, ponds in Chinese gardens will be considered pretty only when they fit for the nature. Banks would wind naturally and banksides are paved with irregular stones. Some even have giantreeds planted in order to pursue the natural charm. In a relatively large water body, (an area of more than several *mu*) a piece of water area would be chosen to display a view of mist-covered peaceful lake. In a lake not large in size, builders will use irregular stones to pave the bank and thin bamboos, wild vines, red fish and green water plants to decorate the scene. Though a small pond, it can leave an image of boundlessness. Rockery makers do not strive to recreate the actual size, but follow the principles of generalization and extraction to represent the shapes of peak, cliff and mountain stream using rockery—making techniques in order to reflect the natural charm and cultural implications of mountains. One of the techniques is to pile earth into a mound or small hill, emphasizing the presentation

Six Hermits in Bamboo Streams painted by a Ming painter who yearned the happy life of drinking and singing of the six intellectuals including poet Li Bai, who retreated in the bamboo stream in the years of Tianbao in the Tang Dynasty.

of partial landscape of the natural mountains. Visitors can't see the complete view of rolling hills, but they can imagine the magnificent picture of peaks over peaks. The technique of leaving imaginary space greatly broadens the expressive power of stones and rocks.

Garden builders often employ the technique of separation to enrich the landscape graduation. For example, little winding stone bridge was always placed on the pond, or foot rocks were arranged in water paddling spots. By doing these, builders enrich depths of field and spatial levels, displaying a sense of depth and serenity of the lake. The usual decorative walls and long corridors don't obstruct the view completely even though they are built to separate the views. They help to increase the depths of field of the view.

Wandering around in a garden in Suzhou, observant visitors will find that each angle offers fresh visual beauty. The white wall facing the window will be decorated with some bamboo, Japanese banana leaves or rockery to avoid the blankness and directness. Chinese gardeners pay much attention to the harmony between the white color of plaster wall and the rich colors, lights, shadows, shapes of the scenery of the garden, which shows the employment of painting techniques in garden building. In short, gardening benefits from painting and painting embodies poetic mood. To seek the poetic mood and pictorial beauty becomes the most important rule in garden making.

Gathering Scenic Wonders and Historical Sites from all over the Country

Whether in imperial gardens or private gardens, it is always a common practice to introduce the scenic wonders and historical

The winding bridge flying across the water in Shanghai Yu Garden

sites into garden building. Even from the same scenic spot that appears in different gardens, people of later generations will find the same cultural and historical implications.

The "Five Famous Mountains" of China were the representatives of mountains in ancient times. Each mountain had temples built for worshipping the God of Mountain. And this kind of practice was also the remains of the nature worship in early stages of human beings. In private gardens in Suzhou, garden builders often place five "stone peaks" in front of or behind the halls to represent the Five Famous Mountains. The appreciation of mountains and stones was even more popular in the later stage of the Qing Dynasty. Gardeners put small rocks in pots and placed them on the table. Through this way, they introduced the wonders of five mountains into the building.

Scenic spots such as "The Moon Reflected in Three Lakes", "Autumn Moon Hung above Peaceful Lake" in the Garden of Perfect Splendor were modeling after some of the well-known top ten sights of the West Lake in Hangzhou. A tower inside

Jiang Tian Temple that stands on the mountaintop of the Gold Mountain beside the river in Zhenjiang, Jiangsu province is the landmark of Zhenjiang City. The related legend about Lady White Snake fought with the Monk Fahai in order to save her husband is widely-known in China. This legend brings strong cultural tinge to the old temple. So in the Summer Resort in Chengde, a scenic spot imitating the view of the Gold Mountain was built.

In the region south of the Yangzi River, whenever March 3rd of lunar calendar comes, people would go on excursions to suburbs. More than 40 scholars including famed calligrapher Wang Xizhi (303–361) would travel to the Orchid Pavilion outside Shaoxing, Zhejiang province. Sitting scattered beside the canals of running water, they placed their wine cups into water and let them flow freely. When a wine cup stopped in front of a certain person, this person must finish the wine first and then make an extemporaneous poem. This process repeated until the wine was finished. Poems they made that day would be collected into a volume with a prefacing from Wang Xizhi. Later these poems were engraved onto stone tablets and placed in the Orchid Pavilion. So not only the Orchid Pavilion in Shaoxing became one famous scenic spot, the practice of drinking wine and chanting poems beside the running water was frequently followed. Inspired by its symbolic implications, Garden builders built flowing-cup pavilions in the Garden of the Peace and Longevity Palace in the Forbidden City and the Summer Resort in Chengde, but the natural running water canals beside the Orchid Pavilion in the old days became the winding water canals engraved on the floor of the pavilion. With these famed scenes being introduced into the garden, their cultural and historical implications were also introduced into the garden. They not only create scenic views in the garden, but also enrich the cultural and artistic realm of the garden.

The yellow wall and the bamboo shadow in the religious Ling Gu Temple in Nanjing

The new twig grown from the old plum tree in the courtyard of old temple in the Tiantai Mountain

Building Temples, Streets and Taverns

Temples are always an indispensable part of Chinese gardens, especially imperial gardens. On one side, this is because of emperors' belief in Buddhism, and on the other side because of the unique views that religious temples create. Sometimes temples could become the major scenes or the center of garden composition. The tranquility and serenity of temples create an unearthly atmosphere.

The Everlasting Blessing Temple and its Lama Tower were built in the Jade Flower Islet in the North Sea Park. The Tower of Buddhist Incense and the Sea of Wisdom Hall in the Summer Palace were built on the south mountainside and ridge of the Longevity Hill. These Buddhist-style structures are the landmark and the center of garden composition of these two imperial gardens because of their outstanding views and unique locations. To the east of Xu Mi Ling Jing Temple in the middle of the rear part of the Longevity Hill in the Summer Palace, there stands a temple named Hua Cheng Ge, which is not large in size. Inside the temple, there is a small-scale octagonal glazed tile pagoda. Windbells hung under the eaves of each floor of the pagoda will chime when wind blows over, displaying an unworldly atmosphere.

Contrasting with the building intentions of the above structures, the Shopping Street in the Houxi River in the Summer Palace created a real scene of worldly life for emperors who were isolated from the outside world—shops standing side by side and shop signs swaying in the wind. Though an artificial scene, it displayed garden owners' yearning toward busy city life. Walking inside, one as if sees the bustle of the waterside street in Suzhou or hears the songs from the Qin Huai River in Nanjing, which stirs great interests of visitors.

It is through the above means that the artistic realm of garden is pregnant with rich meanings. A highly-developed classical art form blending poetry, painting, calligraphy, carving, bonsai, music and traditional opera, Chinese gardening also participates in the creating of the traditional Chinese cultural environment and atmosphere. The refined, exquisite, lyric, graceful and restrained artistic style not only displays a life attitude, but also condenses the Chinese traditional artistic spirit which is influenced by the oriental philosophy. Only after understanding these implications, one can fully appreciate the beauty of classic Chinese gardens.

View-watching Angles

Watching in Motion and Observing Fixedly

There are two ways to appreciate the Chinese garden— watching in motion and observing fixedly. The best way to appreciate small gardens is observing fixedly, but big gardens usually have long visiting routes, so it's better to visit and enjoy

Looking into the distance from the Ji Chang Garden and enjoying the borrowing scene of the Xi Mountain

while moving.

Observing fixedly means that visitors stop to watch the static beauty of gardens. Vantage points suitable for fixed observing are spots like halls, water pavilions, towers, storied buildings, pavilions or terraces. These places offer vast fields of vision and the best views of gardens. When visiting in a garden, one either sits or stays to count the number of fish in the pond or enjoy the cool breeze and bright moon in the pavilion. Each pictorial beauty entering your eyes, such as shadows of flowers moving on the walls or peaks framed into windows, is worth appreciating and enjoying silently.

Visiting routes of garden are mostly winding naturally and

rolling up and down. Some are beside the water, some are located at the foot of hill and others have winding long corridors to shelter the rain and strong sunshine. Winding corridors, rolling stonestep roads or zigzag mountain paths are all good places for watching in motion and enjoying the shifting

The scene framed by the window looks like a landscape painting in scholar's garden

beauty of garden—each move offers visitors fresh visual surprises. In a Chinese garden, primary and supporting views are usually clearly demarcated and scenes varied, so garden builders often design a best visiting route, which connects harmoniously all those best view-watching spots and structures for rest, banqueting, holding activities and residing. Even for those relatively static scenic sights, their views will change when watching angles change. Visitors will be touched by the beauty of rhythms when the beautiful views unfold gradually like a painting.

framing the scenery
In a Chinese garden, doors, windows, caves of a building and trees all combined to form an *outside frame*, circumscribing the views of faraway landscape and artificial scenery. This way of landscaping is called *framing the scenery*.

Providing aesthetical enjoyment whether looking up or looking down.

Garden composition emphasizes the spatial change. While making rockery, creating water views or arranging structures, flowers and trees, gardeners all strive for creating an effect of irregularity with changing heights, which could provide aesthetical enjoyments whether looking up or looking down. Strolling in a garden, one could look up to enjoy the

The Summer Mountain in the Ge Garden

vastness of sky or overlook to enjoy the remoteness of views down below following the changes of landforms or structural heights. The garden is full of charm and wit as each change of angle offers fresh visual beauty.

In the Summer Palace in Beijing, the Buddhist Incense Tower in front of the Longevity Hill towers on the hillside, occupying the commanding point of the garden. The tower will look magnificent when visitors look up. Climbing up and overlooking from the tower, visitors will then be impressed by the panoramic view of the vast lake with ripples dancing above. The Ji Xiao Mountain Villa in Yangzhou also fully made use of this witty technique. Gardeners connected the whole garden through two-floor corridor and mountain paths, which formed a three-dimensional visiting route with landscapes and structures complementing each other.

Fully Activate all Sensory Perception

Visiting in a Chinese classical garden, visitors could not only see beautiful scenes, but also hear the agreeable singing of streams and sweet chirping of orioles and insects. Aroma of peach and plum blossoms in spring, faint scent of lotus in summer, sweet smell of orange osmanthus in autumn and delicate fragrance of calyx canthus in winter are all good enjoyments for sense of smell. In addition, vernal spring breeze blowing gently through willows and sometimes through one's face also gives visitors a very tender and delicate feeling.

The famed scene of "rain dropping on Japanese banana" has evolved into a rhetorical literary quotation. In days of overcast and cloudy, it will be a very special experience to savour the taste of solitude

Looking at Jade Spring Hill from a distance

and serenity alone while listening to the silvery sound of rain dropping on the wide and big Japanese banana leaves. The Listening to Rain Hall in the Humble Administrator's Garden in Suzhou is also related with this artistic realm. The soughing of the wind in the pines planted beside the pavilion will also make people feel a sense of vastness and tranquility. The Pine Wind Pavilion in the Humble Administrator's Garden was named after this implication. So planting pines for listening to wind and growing Japanese banana for listening to rain, become important features of Chinese garden designing.

Different Beauties in Different Seasons

While appreciating garden scenery, one should pay attention to the change of views following the change of lights, seasons, and weathers. It is through the change of weathers that the Jia

The red wall and the old cypress trees complement each other in the Cao Xi Temple Garden in Yunnan

Qing Xi Yu Kuai Xue Pavilion (Fine Sunny Day, Happy Rain and Pleasant Snow Pavilion) in the Lingering Garden in Suzhou stirs feelings of visitors and stresses an optimistic life attitude. The Moon Arrives and Wind Comes Pavilion in the Master-of-Nets Garden in Suzhou would present different views of "first sun rays in the morning" and "rosy clouds at dusk" in one day. From the pavilion, one could see that views of the garden are reflected in the clear water of the pool. The poetic realm of pavilion changes following the change of weather in one day. When bright moon hangs in the sky, the moonlight, lamplight and pool water will reflect each other, displaying a beauty that can't be described by words. In different seasons, scenic views will present different beauties. Beauty that varies due to seasonal change is emphasized and strengthened. In the Ge Garden in Yangzhou, gardeners made rockery imitating the different

The Glasses Lake in former imperial Jing Yi Garden in Beijing Fragrant Hills. This is the winter landscape in the garden.

views of mountains in four seasons, and named "Four Season Rockery." Among the top ten scenic views of Hangzhou, the first four views—"Spring comes into Su Dyke", "Dancing Lotus in the Qu Courtyard", "Autumn Moon in Peaceful Lake" and "Broken Bridge Covered with Snow"—exactly embody the beauties in four seasons.

The Tragedy and Revival
of the Famed Gardens

In ancient China, almost every dynasty went in for large-scale constructions of gardens and palaces at the beginning of the establishment of the new state political power. But most of these gardens were burned down by subverters when the power was overthrown. The rise and decline of gardens was often closely related with the fate of the dynasty. Looking back to the historical progression of human being, countless splendid architectural treasures including the Hanging Garden of ancient Babylon and the Garden of Perfect Splendor were destroyed overnight. Human being's greed and ignorance caused one tragedy after another in the history of civilization.

In 1860, the British and French allied troops invaded into Beijing. In the face of these magnificent gardens and palaces, invaders became looters. The headquarters of allied troops sent down the notice that "everyone could plunder freely". More than ten thousand officers and soldiers rushed into the garden and looted the treasures without restraint. After reaving all treasures

The once destroyed marble boat now anchors at the banks forever

Harmonious and quiet landscape constituted by the Longevity Hill and the Kunming Lake viewed from West Dike eastward

and cultural relics that could be taken away, they sent 3500 people to set fire in every palace and burnt down the Garden of Perfect Splendor, the "garden of gardens." The fire lasted two days and two nights. Days after, the invading army again set fire on the Garden of Clear Ripples, the Jing Yi Garden in the Fragrant Hills, the Jing Ming Garden in the Jade Spring Hill and nearby gardens of grant and private gardens. So many magnificent imperial gardens reflecting the highest achievements in Chinese gardening, and a huge unrivalled garden zone formed after hundreds of years' operation and management were destroyed and burnt into ruins within a period of less than twenty days.

After the looting, the Qing government once ordered the rebuilding of the Garden of Perfect Splendor, but failed because of the lack of fiscal resources and the disagreements from the court officials. In the 14th year of Guang Xu (1888), the Garden of Clear Ripples was partly renovated and was renamed the Pleasant Harmony Garden serving as the imperial resort of Empress Cixi who spent the rest of her life here. In 1900, the Eight Nation's Allied Troops invaded into Beijing, and the Garden of Perfect Splendor, which was already ruins of broken walls, was once again plundered. The invaders from Britain, Russia and Italy had garrisoned in the Garden of Pleasant Harmony for more than one year, during which the precious relics were looted and the structures were destroyed. In 1902, in order to celebrate her 70th birthday, Empress Cixi even started to renovate the Garden of Pleasant Harmony using money that was supposed to strengthen the navy. Due to the frequent damage and the decline of national power of the Qing Dynasty, the weak Qing government had no strength to protect these precious gardens any more.

Among all gardens, the damage upon the Garden of Perfect Splendor was the most severe and devastating. Besides being looted and razed twice by invaders, the garden was also destroyed and robbed by malfeasants, army ruffians and floating peasants. The ruined garden simply became a stone quarry, especially during the Republic of China period (1911–1949) when nobody looked after the ruins of garden and the carriage for carrying the stolen items was one after another during that ten to twenty years. A garden full of structures in old days only has limited numbers of broken walls, pillars and bricks left now. Any stone ornamental pillars and stone lions that were in good condition were taken away. Later, many working units and peasants moved into the garden resulting in the construction of many new buildings. And because that many dykes and banks were dug, trees were fallen, and lakes were changed into rice

The glass pagoda in the Zhao Temple in the Fragrant Hills

field, even the desolate original environment of the scenic spots was gone.

The development of human being's civilization is based on mutual understanding, tolerance and respect. Famous gardens, being plundered and razed are not only the disasters of the civilization, but also the shame of human beings. To protect gardens and cultural relics are human being's collective responsibility.

In 1949, the People's Republic of China was founded and since then China has entered into another new age of history. The classic gardens all over the country have been receiving proper preserving, renovating, maintaining and rebuilding.

The restored Guan Xi Garden in the Jing Yi Garden

Because the Mountainous Summer Resort in Chengde, the largest imperial garden in China, occupied a large space and lacked uniform management, many unrelated organizations and units once stationed inside the garden. A small number of villas and houses were built in the mountainous landscape area and some shops, restaurants and reception houses were built inside the plain and lakes area. Aiming to change the chaotic condition, the local government supported by the national cultural relics protection department carried out the project of clearing up and reorganizing. Through management, the water in the resort becomes clean, trees turn green, the primitive simplicity of the structures is maintained, the grass is as thick as blankets, and the mountain is as lush as before. The Summer Resort of old days once again appears in front of people's eyes. In addition, the Chengde government made great efforts on renovating the eight temples surrounding the resort. The destroyed parts were restored using the traditional techniques. In 1994, the Mountainous Summer Resort in Chengde and the surrounding temples as an integrated architectural group was added in the World Cultural Heritage List by UNESCO.

The Summer Palace was the most well pre-served one among all gardens located in northwest suburbs of Beijing. For the past 50 years, after several times of digging and dredging up of the Kunming Lake, a new water-visiting route has formed because of the abundance of Chang River's water resource. The structures inside the garden were renovated many times, so that they could still keep its magnificence of imperial architecture. After years' painstaking efforts on maintaining, the Summer Palace was listed in the World Cultural Heritage by UNESCO in 1998.

For the past century, most of the former scenic spots and structures of the Jing Yi Garden in the Fragrant Hills have been destroyed. After being tidied up, former scenic spots were restored, some scenic structures were rebuilt, and the present outlook of those large-scale scenic spots was maintained. The original mountainous vegetation was kept. When autumn comes, red leaves will cover the Fragrant Hills. The environment and the artistic realm of the former Jing Yi Garden are still maintained.

The contemporary structures in the Jing Yi Garden in the Fragrant Hills

In 1950s, the Beijing government decided to plant trees extensively in the Garden of

The Qiu Xia Garden in Jiading, a South China style garden built in 1970s.

Perfect Splendor and tried to maintain the original environment of the garden through large-scale afforestation. But due to the lack of further procedures, the destroying activities didn't stop. In the 1980s, the east part of the garden after a little cleaning up was opened to the public as the Park of Ruins of the Garden of Perfect Splendor. In more than ten years from then on, peasants and residents living inside the garden had been moved out step by step. Rice fields were given up, and the scenic spots were restored. The renovation of the scenic spots in the Sea of Happiness and the Yi Chun Garden received special attention, so that some pavilions and water pavilions were rebuilt. In the site of the former Western Storied Building in the Chang Chun Garden, many destroyed architectural parts in old years were excavated. After being cleaned up, the Western Storied Building began to present its original outlook. In recent years, the Beijing government, by considering the opinions from all sides, drafted the developing plan for the Garden of Perfect Splendor based on the actual situation. The main contents of the plan include fully cleaning up the water body, canals, dykes, hills and roads, and then rebuilding some main scenic spots. The plan strives to display parts of the landscapes of the former imperial garden. With this plan, the protection and construction of the Garden of Perfect Splendor are more likely to experience a fast developing period. Hopefully with constant practice and research, the Garden of Perfect Splendor, a masterpiece in an era, could obtain proper protection and be vibrated with life again.

Appendix:
Chronological Table of the Chinese Dynasties

The Paleolithic Period	Approx. 1,700,000–10,000 years ago
The Neolithic Age	Approx. 10,000–4,000 years ago
Xia Dynasty	2070–1600 BC
Shang Dynasty	1600–1046 BC
Western Zhou Dynasty	1046–771 BC
Spring and Autumn Period	770–476 BC
Warring States Period	475–221 BC
Qin Dynasty	221–206 BC
Western Han Dynasty	206 BC–AD 25
Eastern Han Dynasty	25–220
Three Kingdoms	220–280
Western Jin Dynasty	265–317
Eastern Jin Dynasty	317–420
Northern and Southern Dynasties	420–589
Sui Dynasty	581–618
Tang Dynasty	618–907
Five Dynasties	907–960
Northern Song Dynasty	960–1127
Southern Song Dynasty	1127–1279
Yuan Dynasty	1206–1368
Ming Dynasty	1368–1644
Qing Dynasty	1616–1911
Republic of China	1912–1949
People's Republic of China	Founded in 1949